Mindfulness

Harnessing Mindfulness for Business Success

(Using Mindfulness Techniques to Attract Abundance and Happiness)

Matthew Reeves

Published By **Chris David**

Matthew Reeves

All Rights Reserved

Mindfulness: Harnessing Mindfulness for Business Success (Using Mindfulness Techniques to Attract Abundance and Happiness)

ISBN 978-1-7770663-2-1

No part of this guidebook shall be reproduced in any form without permission in writing from the publisher except in the case of brief quotations embodied in critical articles or reviews.

Legal & Disclaimer

The information contained in this book is not designed to replace or take the place of any form of medicine or professional medical advice. The information in this book has been provided for educational & entertainment purposes only.

The information contained in this book has been compiled from sources deemed reliable, and it is accurate to the best of the Author's knowledge; however, the Author cannot guarantee its accuracy and validity and cannot be held liable for any errors or omissions. Changes are periodically made to this book. You must consult your doctor or get professional medical advice before using any of the suggested remedies, techniques, or information in this book.

Upon using the information contained in this book, you agree to hold harmless the Author from and against any damages, costs, and expenses, including any legal fees potentially resulting from the application of any of the information provided by this guide. This disclaimer applies to any damages or injury caused by the use and application, whether directly or indirectly, of any advice or information presented, whether for breach of contract, tort, negligence, personal injury, criminal intent, or under any other cause of action.

You agree to accept all risks of using the information presented inside this book. You need to consult a professional medical practitioner in order to ensure you are both able and healthy enough to participate in this program.

Table Of Contents

Chapter 1: What It Is And Why It Matters 1

Chapter 2: Understanding How It Works . 7

Chapter 3: Mindfulness 82

Chapter 4: Beginner's Thoughts 114

Chapter 5: Awareness 152

Chapter 6: Anchoring 173

Chapter 1: What It Is And Why It Matters

Mindfulness is a exercising that has been round for hundreds of years, however has acquired renewed interest in contemporary years due to its capability to lessen stress, growth properly-being, and enhance regular high-quality of lifestyles. But what exactly is mindfulness, and why is it so vital?

At its center, mindfulness is the exercise of being sincerely present and conscious within the 2d, without judgment or distraction. It entails paying attention to the sensations in our our bodies, our thoughts and feelings, and the arena round us, with a enjoy of interest and openness.

When we practice mindfulness, we cultivate a greater feel of calm, readability, and self-recognition, and are better able to reply to the demanding situations of lifestyles with greater information and resilience.

In this chapter, we're able to discover what mindfulness is, how it may advantage us, and a number of the commonplace misconceptions approximately mindfulness that would get inside the way of growing a normal exercise.

Whether you are without a doubt new to mindfulness or have some experience with it already, this monetary catastrophe will lay the foundation for the relaxation of the e-book and offer a sturdy expertise of what mindfulness is and why it subjects.

Defining mindfulness

Mindfulness is the exercise of being present and completely engaged within the modern 2d, without judgment or distraction. It involves listening to one's thoughts, emotions, and bodily sensations in a non-judgmental way, on the same time as furthermore being aware about one's environment. Mindfulness is regularly cultivated thru severa techniques, along side meditation, yoga, or actually taking note of the prevailing 2nd in every day lifestyles.

The final intention of mindfulness is to accumulate a more experience of interest, recognition, and compassion for oneself and others.

Mindfulness has been demonstrated to have numerous benefits, together with reducing pressure, improving highbrow and bodily health, and developing standard well-being.

Benefits of mindfulness exercise

There are many capability blessings of mindfulness exercise, which encompass:

1. Stress discount: Mindfulness has been validated to lessen the stages of the stress hormone cortisol, supporting to decrease ordinary strain degrees.

2. Improved highbrow health: Mindfulness has been found to be an powerful remedy for despair, anxiety, and unique highbrow fitness conditions, and might decorate traditional temper and properly-being.

three. Better sleep: Practicing mindfulness can help calm the thoughts and decrease racing thoughts, making it a whole lot less tough to go to sleep and stay asleep.

4. Increased popularity and productivity: By growing interest and lowering distraction, mindfulness can help enhance popularity and productiveness in each day life.

five. Improved physical fitness: Mindfulness has been validated to improve severa bodily health conditions, together with chronic pain, excessive blood stress, and irritable bowel syndrome (IBS).

6. Enhanced relationships: Mindfulness can help enhance conversation and empathy in relationships, main to better connections with others.

7. Increased self-reputation: Through mindfulness practice, humans can boom a extra experience of self-cognizance and discover ways to better recognize their very private thoughts, emotions, and behaviors.

Overall, mindfulness exercise can help people lead a greater satisfactory and balanced life by way of the use of decreasing strain, improving intellectual and physical health, and developing average nicely-being.

Common misconceptions about mindfulness

There are severa commonplace misconceptions about mindfulness that can get inside the way of growing a everyday exercising. Some of those misconceptions encompass:

1. Mindfulness is satisfactory for religious or religious talents: While mindfulness has its roots in splendid non secular and spiritual traditions, it isn't always inherently tied to any character belief system. Mindfulness can be practiced thru simply everyone, no matter their religious or non secular beliefs.

2. Mindfulness is first-rate approximately relaxation: While mindfulness can help lessen stress and increase rest, it isn't always pretty tons feeling calm and peaceful. Mindfulness is

also about being present with some thing goes on within the moment, whether or not or no longer it is outstanding, ugly, or neutral.

three. Mindfulness is clearly too difficult or time-ingesting: Mindfulness may be practiced in masses of unique procedures, and does no longer have to be hard or time-eating. Even brief durations of mindfulness exercise at some stage inside the day may have widespread blessings.

four. Mindfulness is ready emptying the mind: Mindfulness isn't about emptying the mind or searching out to save you mind altogether. Rather, it is approximately being aware about mind and exquisite intellectual hobby with out getting caught up in them.

Chapter 2: Understanding How It Works

While mindfulness has been practiced for thousands of years, it has first-class been inside the previous couple of a long term that researchers have started to discover the underlying mechanisms of strategies it works.

Through research the use of thoughts imaging, behavioral tests, and tremendous strategies, scientists have started out to understand the techniques in which mindfulness can effect our brains and our bodies, and the manner the ones adjustments bring about the severa advantages that we partner with mindfulness workout.

In this financial ruin, we're able to discover the scientific research within the once more of mindfu ness, and the manner it influences our brains, our our our our bodies, and our accepted properly-being. We will delve into the unique thoughts areas and networks which may be activated within the direction of mindfulness workout, and the modifications that arise in those regions over the years.

We may even speak the numerous physiological and mental results of mindfulness, and the way they could assist us control strain, beautify our temper, and beautify our common fine of life.

Whether you're a novice to mindfulness or have a few experience with the practice, this bankruptcy will offer valuable belief into the generation inside the back of mindfulness, and why it has grow to be this sort of popular and powerful technique to improving our fitness and properly-being.

Types of meditation practices.

There are numerous taken into consideration one of a type forms of meditation practices that individuals can discover, relying on their goals and options. Here are a number of the most common kinds of meditation:

1. Mindfulness meditation: This is the most well-known form of meditation, and includes

that specialize within the present 2d and looking one's mind and sensations without judgment.

Mindfulness meditation can be practiced thru loads of strategies, in conjunction with breath reputation, body scanning, or focusing on a particular phrase or phrase.

2. Transcendental meditation: This form of meditation includes repeating a mantra or sound to assist calm the thoughts and acquire a rustic of deep relaxation.

3. Loving-kindness meditation: Also called Metta meditation, this exercise includes that specialize in sending loving-kindness and compassion to oneself and others, which includes loved ones or perhaps hard humans.

4. Body take a look at meditation: This shape of meditation includes bringing awareness to every part of the frame, starting from the top of the pinnacle and running all of the manner all the way down to the ft. This can help release physical anxiety and promote rest.

5. Movement meditation: This involves schooling mindfulness at the same time as transferring the frame, together with thru yoga, strolling meditation, or Tai Chi. This may be an first rate choice for individuals who discover it hard to take a seat down down despite the fact that for prolonged periods of time.

6. Chakra meditation: This form of meditation focuses on balancing the power facilities in the frame, or chakras, through visualization and respiratory strategies.

There are many distinct forms of meditation practices available, and it can be useful to find out some one-of-a-kind strategies to discover what works fantastic for you.

Ultimately, the purpose of any meditation exercising is to promote a country of internal calm and popularity, and to domesticate more self-recognition and compassion.

Mindfulness meditation instructions.

Here are a few fundamental commands for mindfulness meditation:

1. Find a quiet and snug location wherein you may take a seat down or lie down without being disturbed.

2. Set a timer on your preferred duration of exercising (e.g. F ve minutes, 10 minutes, and 15 mines).

3. Close your eyes and take some deep breaths, allowing yourself to lighten up and allow flow into of any anxiety to your body.

4. Bring your interest to your breath, noticing the sensations of every inhale and exhale. You can also focus at the upward thrust and fall of your chest or the sensation of air shifting interior and from your nostrils.

5. When your mind wanders (and it'll), in reality examine the idea or distraction, after which lightly guide your attention decrease back to your breath. You may additionally additionally find it beneficial to label the

distraction as "questioning" or "feeling" earlier than returning to the breath.

6. Repeat this machine within the course of your meditation, staying as gift and centered as you can. Remember that the motive isn't to eliminate thoughts, but to without a doubt have a have a look at them without getting stuck up in them.

7. When the timer goes off, take some deep breaths and convey your interest decrease back in your frame and your environment.

As you still workout mindfulness meditation, you could locate it useful to test with special techniques, which consist of body scanning, walking meditation, or focusing on a particular word or phrase.

Remember to be affected person with yourself, as developing a normal meditation exercising can take time and workout.

Starting and maintaining a meditation exercise can be difficult, however right proper here are a few hints that will help you get began and live devoted:

1. Start small: Begin with just a few minutes of meditation every day, and gradually boom the duration as you turn out to be more comfortable with the exercise.

2. Make it a habit: Choose a specific time and location in your meditation practice, and try to preserve on with this recurring as masses as viable. This can help create a sense of consistency and make it simpler to shape a dependency.

3. Set realistic goals: Don't assume to experience profound modifications or insights at once. Remember that meditation is a long-term practice, and development can take time.

four. Find a method that works for you: Experiment with particular types of meditation, and find out the most effective that resonates with you the most. This can assist make the exercise experience greater fun and gratifying.

5. Be affected person with yourself: Meditation can be tough, and it is everyday to enjoy distractions, pain, and resistance. Try not to select yourself for these research, and as a substitute technique them with interest and compassion.

6. Use guided meditations: If you discover it hard to meditate in your personal, strive using guided meditations or apps that can offer shape and assist.

7. Join a community: Consider becoming a member of a meditation agency or elegance, or finding a meditation friend who can help maintain you accountable and caused.

Remember that the advantages of meditation are cumulative, and the extra you exercising, the greater you're likely to revel in the effective effects.

By starting small, locating a technique that works for you, and staying steady, you could increase a meditation exercise that supports your mental, emotional, and physical properly-being.

03 Mindful Breathing: Using the Breath to Cultivate Mindfulness

In this bankruptcy we are able to popularity on sensible techniques for integrating mindfulness into your every day existence.

While mindfulness meditation is a treasured tool for cultivating gift-second consciousness and lowering stress, the blessings of mindfulness can enlarge a ways past your meditation cushion.

By getting to know the way to deliver mindfulness into your regular sports activities, you could experience greater ease, clarity, and pride on your each day lifestyles.

We will find out some of easy and practical strategies to exercising mindfulness in the course of your day, whether or no longer you are at artwork, at domestic, or out within the worldwide.

Mindful breathing is a easy and powerful approach for cultivating mindfulness for your every day lifestyles. By bringing your interest on your breath, you can anchor your self in the gift second and amplify a greater enjoy of calm and readability.

To exercise conscious breathing, find out a comfortable feature wherein you could sit down down down or lie down with out being disturbed.

Close your eyes or decrease your gaze, and begin to be privy to your breath.

Notice the sensation of the air moving outside and inside of your nostrils, or the upward push and fall of your chest with each inhale and exhale.

As you focus for your breath, you may phrase that your thoughts starts offevolved offevolved to wander.

Thoughts, emotions, and sensations may moreover furthermore upward thrust up, pulling your interest faraway from the breath.

When this takes place, simply broadly recognized the distraction, and lightly guide your interest decrease lower back to the breath.

You may also find out it beneficial to label the distraction as "questioning" or "feeling" in advance than returning to the breath, as this may help you permit circulate of the distraction and are available again to the present 2d.

As you still exercise conscious breathing, you can find that your thoughts turns into more calm and targeted. You can also moreover word a more experience of relaxation and ease to your frame.

With normal practice, conscious respiratory will let you expand more self-recognition, lessen strain and tension, and beautify your everyday well-being.

In the subsequent section, we are able to find out the manner to deliver conscious breathing into your every day existence, so that you can exercising mindfulness in some of situations and environments.

The importance of the breath in mindfulness

The breath is a foundational detail of mindfulness workout, as it offers a tangible and constant anchor in your hobby. By focusing at the breath, you could deliver your interest into the triumphing 2d, it actually is vital for cultivating mindfulness.

In addition to providing a focal point in your hobby, the breath is in element associated for your physiological and emotional states. When you are burdened or traumatic, as an instance, your breath has a tendency to grow to be shallow and rapid.

By consciously slowing and deepening your breath, you can spark off the frame's relaxation response, that could help lessen pressure and anxiety.

The breath moreover offers treasured information approximately your u . S . Of mind and frame. By tuning into the first-rate and rhythm of your breath, you may benefit notion into your emotional and physical states.

For instance, in case you phrase that your breath is shallow and uneven, you may recognize that you are feeling annoying or beaten. By being attentive to those cues, you could respond extra skillfully on your very very very own wishes and make picks that aid your properly-being.

By growing a extra interest of your breath, you can also enhance your potential to live centered and observed on your each day lifestyles.

Rather than getting caught up inside the distractions and pressures of the outdoor worldwide, you could return to the breath as a touchstone in your interest, bringing your self again to the prevailing 2d and cultivating a greater feel of peace and clarity.

Simple respiratory physical sports for mindfulness

There are many particular respiratory physical activities as a manner to assist you to domesticate mindfulness to your each day lifestyles. Here are some easy bodily games to get you started:

1. Counted breaths: Begin by way of sitting or mendacity down in a snug characteristic. Close your eyes and start to breathe deeply and slowly. As you inhale, rely to 4 for your mind.

As you exhale, remember range to 6. Repeat this sample for several mins, allowing your breath to gradual and deepen with each cycle.

2. Belly respiration: Find a snug characteristic wherein you could sit down down or lie down without being disturbed. Place one hand for your stomach, and the alternative hand on your chest. Take a deep breath in via your nose, filling your stomach with air.

As you exhale, allow your stomach lighten up and launch the air. Repeat this pattern for numerous minutes, that specialize within the feeling of the breath moving outside and inside of your body.

3. Box respiratory: Begin thru finding a snug seated function. Inhale deeply for a count number of 4, hold your breath for a count number of four, exhale for a depend of 4, after which hold your breath for a recall of 4.

Repeat this pattern for numerous mins, feeling the calming outcomes of the rhythmic respiratory.

4. Mindful taking walks: Walking additionally may be a effective manner to exercise mindfulness. As you stroll, recognition on the sensation of your feet touching the floor, the motion of your frame, and the rhythm of your breath.

If your thoughts starts offevolved to wander, gently guide your interest decrease lower back for your breath and the sensations of taking walks.

These sports activities sports are only a few examples of the numerous strategies you may use respiratory to domesticate mindfulness. The key is to find a way that works for you, and to exercise frequently to growth your mindfulness muscle.

With time and constant try, you can enjoy more calm, readability, and nicely-being to your each day life.

Techniques for integrating aware respiratory into every day life

Integrating conscious respiration into your daily lifestyles can be tough earlier than the entirety, but with workout, it could emerge as a natural a part of your routine.

Here are a few techniques you can use to make mindfulness a everyday part of your day:

1. Schedule conscious breathing breaks: Set apart particular instances sooner or later of the day to recognition for your breath, although it's handiest for a couple of minutes at a time. You can try this in the course of

your flow backward and forward, finally of a ruin at paintings, or earlier than mattress.

2. Use breath as an anchor: Throughout the day, use your breath as an anchor to deliver your self returned to the winning second. When you find out your thoughts wandering, take a few deep breaths and bring your interest decrease lower back to the mission accessible.

3. Mindful transitions: Use the transition amongst obligations or sports to take some deep breaths and convey your reputation again to the prevailing second. This will assist you to transition greater effortlessly between duties and decrease strain.

4. Set intentiors: Before beginning a project, take a 2nd to set an goal for the way you want to technique it. Take some deep breaths and reputation in your goal before starting the assignment.

5. Combine with different sports activities: You can also combine aware respiration with

tremendous sports, which incorporates yoga or workout. Focus to your breath as you drift through the poses or sports, and permit your breath guide your movements.

Remember that integrating mindful respiration into your every day life is a exercising, and it takes time to growth. Be affected person with yourself and preserve operating toward, even if you most effective have a couple of minutes a day to commit to it.

Over time, you can discover that mindfulness will become a herbal and to be had part of your each day everyday.

four. Mindful Movement: Bringing Mindfulness into Physical Activity

Physical hobby is an critical a part of a wholesome life-style, and can have severa advantages for our physical, intellectual, and emotional nicely-being.

However, whilst we method exercise as a chore or a manner to an stop, we also can pass over out on the numerous rewards that come from transferring our our our our bodies with hobby and cause.

Mindful movement is a exercise that consists of bringing mindfulness to physical pastime, whether or not or not it is thru yoga, walking, trekking, or a few different shape of motion. By cultivating recognition of our frame, breath, and surroundings, we're capable of deepen our connection to our bodily selves, lessen pressure and tension, and enhance our essential enjoy of well-being.

In this financial disaster, we are going to discover the benefits of aware motion, strategies for incorporating mindfulness into bodily interest, and techniques for growing a extra conscious and fun approach to exercise.

Whether you're an professional athlete or certainly starting out, aware motion will will let you tap into the transformative electricity of physical interest, and revel in the severa joys of moving with purpose and awareness.

The blessings of mixing mindfulness and bodily hobby

Combining mindfulness and physical interest can also have many blessings for our physical, mental, and emotional properly-being.

Here are a number of the techniques that mindfulness can decorate our revel in of bodily pastime:

1. Increased attention: Mindfulness lets in us stay gift in the second, that can enhance our functionality to awareness at some point of physical hobby.

By bringing our interest to our breath, frame, and environment, we are able to track out distractions and live engaged in our interest.

2. Reduced strain and anxiety: Physical hobby is a exquisite way to reduce stress and tension, and mindfulness can beautify this impact.

By bringing recognition to our frame and breath, we're able to launch anxiety and calm the mind, fundamental to greater relaxation and a feel of well-being.

3. Enhanced performance: Mindfulness can assist us faucet into our frame's natural abilties and acquire top performance.

By staying centered and conscious, we are able to better connect to our body, music in to our strength levels, and make modifications to optimize our typical performance.

4. Improved body cognizance: Mindful movement can beautify our body interest, helping us higher understand our bodily boundaries and dreams.

By tuning into our breath and bodily sensations, we're able to higher track into our frame's indicators, and make selections that guide our health and properly-being.

five. Increased amusement: Finally, combining mindfulness and bodily interest can actually make exercising more a laugh.

By bringing cognizance to the enjoy, we are able to have amusing with the physical sensations, take pride in our accomplishments, and locate greater joy and fulfillment in moving our our bodies.

Overall, the advantages of mixing mindfulness and bodily interest are numerous, and can help us live greater healthful, happier lives.

By incorporating mindfulness into our physical hobby, we're able to rework exercising from a chore or duty into a satisfying, nourishing exercising that helps our regular properly-being.

Examples of conscious movement practices

There are many sorts of physical hobby that can be practiced with mindfulness, right here are a few examples of conscious motion practices:

1. Yoga: Yoga is a workout that includes bodily postures, breath manage, and meditation. Practicing yoga with mindfulness consists of bringing interest to the frame,

breath, and sensations, and focusing on the prevailing 2nd.

2. Running or taking walks: Running or on foot may be a fantastic way to comprise mindfulness into physical hobby. By focusing at the breath and bodily sensations, runners can domesticate a revel in of mindfulness and presence in some unspecified time inside the destiny of their exercise.

3. Walking: Walking is a clean, available form of physical interest that may be practiced with mindfulness. By tuning into the sensations of the body, the breath, and the surroundings, walkers can experience a experience of rest and peace.

4. Tai chi or qigong: Tai chi and qigong are practices that include sluggish, mild actions, mixed with respiration and visualization strategies. Practicing those moves with mindfulness can assist lessen pressure, enhance stability and versatility, and enhance not unusual nicely-being.

5. Dance: Dancing may be a amusing and exciting manner to incorporate mindfulness into physical hobby. By tuning into the rhythm of the music, the movement of the frame, and the breath, dancers can enjoy a experience of flow and pleasure.

6. Swimming: Swimming is a low-effect shape of bodily hobby that can be practiced with mindfulness. By focusing at the breath and the sensations of the frame in the water, swimmers can revel in a enjoy of rest and rejuvenation.

These are only a few examples of aware movement practices. Any shape of physical hobby can be practiced with mindfulness, and with the useful resource of way of bringing focus to the prevailing second, we are capable of rework exercise into a fulfilling, nourishing exercising that helps our normal properly-being.

Tips for incorporating conscious movement into every day exercises

Here are some guidelines for incorporating aware motion into each day workout exercises:

1. Start small: It can be tempting to jump into a new exercising regular with enthusiasm, but it's miles vital to start small and gradually growth your workout. Set small, ability goals, and regu arly increase the intensity or length of your exercising as you revel in snug.

2. Choose an hobby you enjoy: The key to sustaining a regular workout regular is to select out an hobby that you experience. Whether it's miles yoga, strolling, dancing, or swimming, discover an hobby that feels proper to you and that you live up for operating within the direction of.

three. Focus at the triumphing 2d: When practicing aware movement, it's miles critical to live centered on the triumphing second. Bring interest to the bodily sensations for your frame, the breath, and the environment round you. Try to track out distractions and stay gift inside the moment.

four. Make it a addiction: Incorporating aware motion into your each day ordinary is less difficult in case you make it a addiction. Try to exercise on the identical time each day, and set apart a dedicated vicinity on your exercising.

5. Take breaks for the duration of the day: Even in case you do not have time for a whole exercising ordinary, you could notwithstanding the fact that comprise conscious movement into your every day ordinary thru taking breaks for the duration of the day. Take a short stroll across the block, carry out a little moderate stretching, or exercise a few deep respiration carrying events.

6. Find a community: Practicing conscious motion with a hard and fast of like-minded human beings can be a extraordinary way to stay prompted and stimulated. Consider becoming a member of a yoga beauty, strolling institution, or dance network to

connect to others who percentage your passion for aware motion.

Incorporating aware movement into your each day normal can help enhance your physical, intellectual, and emotional nicely-being. By education with popularity and presence, you may redesign exercising right right into a nourishing practice that helps your ordinary health and happiness.

five. Mindful Eating: Bringing Awareness to Food and Eating Habits

In modern day speedy-paced global, it's easy to fall into the trap of senseless consuming. We rush through food, consume at the pass, and frequently find out ourselves snacking on junk food with out even understanding it.

However, with the aid of bringing consciousness to our meals and eating conduct, we can redesign the way we nourish our our our bodies and enjoy more tiers of fitness and nicely-being. In this bankruptcy, we're going to explore the exercising of conscious consuming and the way it will let you amplify a more in shape, greater balanced courting with meals.

We'll cover simple strategies for bringing popularity for your eating behavior, further to recommendations for making healthier meals selections and taking element in your food with greater presence and gratitude.

Whether you are a busy professional, a discern juggling multiple obligations, or in reality a person seeking to domesticate greater mindfulness to your every day life, the exercising of aware eating can be a powerful tool for helping your commonplace properly-being.

The connection amongst mindfulness and food

Mindfulness and meals are interconnected in loads of strategies. Mindful ingesting is a exercise that consists of bringing recognition and interest to the revel in of ingesting, which includes the taste, texture, and smell of food, similarly to the physical sensations and emotions that upward push up at some stage inside the eating technique.

This workout can assist us amplify a deeper connection with our our our bodies, further to a extra expertise of our ingesting behavior and food choices.

Many folks have advanced horrible consuming conduct which might be rooted in mindless ingesting styles. We may consume even as we are not hungry, overeat or undereat, or pick out dangerous elements that do not nourish our our our our bodies.

By walking toward mindfulness in some unspecified time in the future of meals, we are capable of discover ways to track in to our our bodies and make greater conscious selections approximately what we eat and what form of we consume. We also can learn how to have fun with our food and enjoy the enjoy of ingesting, in preference to dashing via meals or mindlessly snacking at some diploma within the day.

In addition to promoting greater wholesome consuming behavior, aware ingesting also can assist us cultivate a deeper experience of gratitude and appreciation for the food we devour.

By bringing cognizance to the supply of our food and the efforts that pass into growing, getting ready, and transporting it, we are able to develop a more experience of connection with the natural worldwide and the folks that offer us with sustenance.

Overall, the connection amongst mindfulness and meals is a effective one, imparting us the opportunity to transform our relationship with meals and increase a extra nourishing, sustainable method to eating.

By schooling conscious eating, we're able to deliver extra cognizance and purpose to our meals picks and expand a deeper revel in of reference to our our our bodies and the world spherical us.

The connection among mindfulness and food

Mindfulness and food are in detail related, and our courting with meals can extensively effect our highbrow and physical nicely-being. The exercising of aware ingesting consists of being gift and absolutely engaged with the experience of eating, bringing interest to the sensations of taste, texture, and aroma, similarly to to the frame's hunger and fullness signals.

When we exercise conscious consuming, we grow to be extra attuned to our our bodies' dreams and are higher prepared to make knowledgeable alternatives about what we eat. This, in turn, can reason extra healthful meals picks and a greater balanced and nourishing food plan.

We moreover become more aware of our eating conduct, at the side of emotional consuming, senseless snacking, or overeating, that could help us to become aware of the underlying causes of these behaviors and enlarge strategies for overcoming them.

In addition to promoting more wholesome ingesting conduct, conscious consuming also can help us to extend a more appreciation for the food we eat and its effect on our our bodies and the sector round us.

By cultivating gratitude and interest for the food we consume, we can increase a deeper enjoy of reference to our our bodies, our businesses, and the herbal international.

Overall, the connection amongst mindfulness and meals is a effective one, supplying us the opportunity to convert our relationship with food and broaden a extra conscious, nourishing method to eating.

By education conscious ingesting, we are able to carry greater focus and cause to our food picks, expand a deeper connection with our our our our bodies and the sector round us, and promote greater fitness and nicely-being.

Mindful eating techniques and sports activities

Here are some conscious consuming strategies and sports activities that you can strive:

1. Slow down and have a laugh together together with your meals: Take a while to consume your meals and be aware about the flavors, smells, and textures of your meals. Chew slowly and have fun with every chew.

2. Focus in your senses: Use all of your senses to explore your food, paying attention to the colours, smells, textures, and tastes.

three. Practice gratitude: Before you begin your meal, take a 2nd to explicit gratitude for the meals in your plate and all and sundry who contributed to its introduction and delivery.

four. Engage in conscious respiration: Take a few deep breaths earlier than eating to middle your self and bring attention to the winning 2d.

5. Use a hunger scale: Check in together with your frame and inspect your hunger diploma

on a scale of 1 to ten, with 1 being very hungry and 10 being very full. This will allow making a decision how lots to eat and avoid overeating.

6. Tune into your frame's indicators: Pay interest on your frame's starvation and fullness cues as you devour, and save you eating at the same time as you experience satisfied as opposed to overly complete.

7. Practice conscious snacking: When you sense the urge to snack, take a moment to pause and study your starvation level earlier than conducting for meals. Choose wholesome snacks and enjoy each bite mindfully.

eight. Experiment with new substances: Try new meals and flavors, and approach every meal with a sense of interest and openness to new studies.

By schooling the ones techniques and wearing activities, you can extend a more aware approach to eating and enhance your relationship with food. Over time, you could discover which you are better capable of music into your frame's goals and make extra knowledgeable choices approximately what and what form of to eat.

How to boom a greater aware relationship with meals and ingesting

Developing a greater conscious courting with meals and consuming includes a aggregate of mindfulness practices and practical strategies that will let you to be extra present and conscious in some unspecified time in the future of mealtimes.

Here are some hints to get you commenced:

1. Practice conscious consuming: As we noted earlier, conscious consuming consists of being truely present and engaged with the enjoy of eating. Take time to pride in and admire the flavors and textures of your food, and be aware about your body's hunger and fullness indicators.

2. Focus on nourishment: Rather than thinking of meals as a supply of pleasure or consolation, approach it as a way of nourishing your body and promoting remaining health and well-being.

three. Create a supportive surroundings: Surround yourself with healthful, nourishing food and create a non violent, relaxing environment for mealtimes.

4. Tune into your frame's dreams: Learn to concentrate to your frame's signs and symptoms, together with hunger, fullness, and cravings, and respond therefore.

five. Practice self-compassion: Be kind and compassionate with your self, spotting that growing a conscious relationship with food is a method that takes time and exercising.

6. Build healthy behavior: Develop healthful conduct spherical mealtimes, such as sitting all of the way all the way down to devour, averting distractions, and taking time to put together healthful food.

7. Seek useful useful resource: Consider strolling with a registered dietitian or therapist who specializes in mindfulness and consuming issues that will help you growth a greater conscious approach to food and ingesting.

By running closer to those strategies and incorporating mindfulness into your each day lifestyles, you could broaden a more aware courting with food and eating that promotes extra fitness and nicely-being.

6. Mindfulness in Daily Life: Applying Mindfulness to Everyday Activities

Incorporating mindfulness into your each day life may be a powerful tool for reducing stress, growing popularity and productivity, and improving popular properly-being. While mindfulness practices like meditation and conscious respiration are truely crucial, it is also critical to apply mindfulness to ordinary sports sports to truely accumulate the blessings.

In this monetary disaster, we are able to find out how you may exercising mindfulness to everyday sports to cultivate a greater experience of presence and interest to your every day life. We may additionally provide practical hints and physical video video games for incorporating mindfulness into each day sports which includes walking, cleaning, and jogging, amongst others.

By the stop of this chapter, you may have a higher information of a way to comply with mindfulness in your every day existence to decorate your ordinary well-being and first-rate of existence.

Techniques for bringing mindfulness into each day sports

Bringing mindfulness into daily sports consists of consciously and deliberately bringing your hobby to the existing second and to the pastime to hand.

Here are a few strategies for incorporating mindfulness into your every day sports:

1. Single-tasking: Focus on one interest at a time, giving it your complete hobby and heading off distractions. For example, in case you are washing dishes, attention on the sensations of the water and cleansing soap on your palms, the sound of the dishes clinking together, and the movements of your fingers and fingers.

2. Savoring: Take time to satisfaction in and admire the memories spherical you, which includes the taste and aroma of your meals or the splendor of nature on a walk.

three. Body focus: Bring your hobby in your body and the sensations you are experiencing, which include the feeling of your ft at the ground or the breath transferring outside and inside of your body.

four. Mindful listening: Listen attentively and with an open mind, absolutely present within the 2d, and preserving off distractions.

five. Mindful respiration: Bring your attention in your breath, specializing inside the sensation of the air transferring indoors and from your body.

6. Mindful strolling: Focus at the bodily sensations of taking walks, together with the feeling of your feet at the ground and the moves of your frame.

7. Non-judgmental recognition: Observe your mind and feelings with interest and with out judgment or criticism.

By incorporating those strategies into your each day activities, you may cultivate extra presence, consciousness, and mindfulness to your regular existence. Start through way of choosing one or sports activities activities every day to exercise mindfulness, and grade by grade enlarge your workout to embody extra sports activities as you grow to be greater snug.

Over time, you can increase extra mindfulness and a deeper appreciation for the opinions of every day life.

Tips for staying conscious within the midst of a busy day

Staying aware at some point of a hectic day can be a project, but it is feasible with workout and attempt.

Here are a few suggestions for staying aware inside the midst of a hectic day:

1. Set reminders: Set reminders to your smartphone or laptop to pause and take some deep breaths or to workout a brief mindfulness workout.

2. Take breaks: Take ordinary breaks sooner or later of the day to stretch, pass your frame, or take a brief stroll to easy your mind and refocus your attention.

three. Mindful transitions: Practice aware transitions amongst responsibilities or sports, bringing your interest honestly to the winning 2nd earlier than transferring straight away to the subsequent challenge.

4. Reduce multitasking: Avoid multitasking as plenty as feasible and attention on one mission at a time, giving it your whole attention.

five. Be determined in conversations: When speakme to others, be absolutely gift in the verbal exchange and keep away from distractions collectively along with your cell cellphone or computer.

6. Accept your feelings: Allow yourself to enjoy your emotions with out judging or trying to suppress them. By acknowledging your emotions and accepting them, you can release them and pass on with greater ease.

7. Practice self-compassion: Be kind to yourself and renowned that you are doing the excellent you can inside the second. Treat your self with the same kindness and compassion you could provide to an top notch pal.

By schooling the ones suggestions and incorporating mindfulness into your daily ordinary, you may boom your capability to live present and centered all through a busy day.

Remember, mindfulness is a abilties that can be developed with workout, so be affected person with yourself and hold at it.

Mindfulness practices for stress bargain and advanced rest

There are many mindfulness practices that may help lesser strain and boom rest.

Here are a few examples:

1. Body scan meditation: This exercising consists of mer dacity down or sitting effects and bringing hobby to each part of the body, one after the alternative, from head to toe. By focusing on the sensations in each part of the body, you can turn out to be more privy to tension and launch it.

2. Progressive muscle relaxation: This approach includes tensing and releasing each muscle organization inside the frame, starting

with the ft and strolling as a great deal as the pinnacle. By deliberately tensing and interesting each muscle, you could launch physical tension and enjoy a revel in of deep rest.

three. Mindful breathing: Simply focusing at the breath can assist calm the thoughts and decrease strain. Try taking some deep breaths, focusing at the sensations of the breath as it actions inside and outside of the body.

four. Visualization: Visualizing a chilled photograph or scene, such as a non violent seaside or a wooded area, can help reduce stress and promote rest.

5. Walking meditation: Walking mindfully, listening to the sensations within the feet and the motion of the frame, can assist reduce strain and growth rest.

6.

These practices can be accomplished on my own or in combination with brilliant mindfulness practices. By often incorporating those practices into your normal, you may boom a extra feel of calm and rest, decreasing stress and promoting conventional well-being.

7. Overcoming Obstacles to Mindfulness: Dealing with Common Challenges

Mindfulness may be a powerful device for reducing stress, growing consciousness, and selling preferred nicely-being. However, like numerous new addiction or capability, mindfulness can come with its personal set of demanding conditions.

In this financial ruin, we can discover some commonplace obstacles to mindfulness and strategies for overcoming them. Whether you're suffering to stay normal at the side of your practice, find out it tough to stay gift inside the 2nd, or are managing distinct commonplace worrying situations, this economic disaster will provide sensible guidelines and techniques for cultivating a greater aware way of being, even within the face of obstacles.

Common challenges in mindfulness exercise

There are numerous not unusual demanding situations that humans can also additionally face on the equal time as trying to establish a mindfulness practice.

These demanding situations can include:

1. Difficulty staying centered: It may be difficult to stay centered on the winning 2d, mainly at the equal time as our minds are constantly pulled in precise recommendations. This can result in frustration and a experience of failure.

2. Lack of time: Many people might also additionally battle to discover the time to exercising mindfulness, in particular in the event that they have a hectic schedule or some of responsibilities.

three. Resistance to change: Some people may moreover resist the idea of mindfulness or find out it tough to trade their conduct and methods of wondering.

4. Self-judgment: It's common to be vital of oneself, particularly at the same time as first starting a mindfulness exercise. This can reason feelings of inadequacy and discouragement.

5. Physical ache: Sitting in a single position for an prolonged time frame can be bodily uncomfortable, mainly for those who are not used to it.

These annoying situations may want to make it tough to installation a ordinary mindfulness practice. However, with endurance and endurance, the ones stressful conditions may be conquer.

In the following sections, we're able to explore strategies for overcoming these demanding situations and establishing a a success mindfulness practice.

Techniques for overcoming obstacles to mindfulness

Here are some strategies for overcoming common barriers to mindfulness:

1. Difficulty staying centered: The key to overcoming hassle staying centered is to technique mindfulness exercising with a non-judgmental attitude. Accept that your mind will wander, and lightly supply your hobby again to the prevailing 2nd whilst you be aware it has wandered.

Additionally, it is able to be helpful to focus on a selected anchor to your hobby, which includes your breath, a legitimate, or a physical sensation.

2. Lack of time: You can start small with the beneficial useful resource of placing apart just a few mins each day for mindfulness exercising, and progressively growth the quantity of time as you turn out to be greater cushty with the practice.

You also can attempt incorporating mindfulness into day by day sports, together with washing dishes or taking a stroll.

three. Resistance to alternate: If you find out yourself proof in opposition to the idea of mindfulness, try and method it with an open thoughts.

Recognize that it takes time and exercising to cultivate mindfulness and that it's far a expertise that may be developed like a few distinct.

four. Self-judgment: Self-judgment may be mainly difficult, but it's vital to undergo in thoughts that mindfulness isn't always approximately achieving perfection. It's about being present and non-judgmental inside the 2d.

When you be aware self-judgment bobbing up, famend it, and lightly carry your interest yet again on your breath or anchor.

five. Physical pain: If you're experiencing physical ache sooner or later of mindfulness workout, attempt adjusting your posture or incorporating moderate motion into your exercise, together with stretching or yoga.

Remember that mindfulness is a practice, and it is normal to experience challenges along the manner. By staying affected person, chronic, and compassionate with your self, you can triumph over those barriers and installation a successful mindfulness exercise.

How to keep a mindfulness exercise over time

Maintaining a mindfulness exercise over the years calls for dedication, location, and a willingness to conform.

Here are a few guidelines for preserving a mindfulness practice:

1. Set practical dreams: Start with a small purpose it absolutely is viable, which includes practicing for 5-10 minutes an afternoon. Gradually boom the period of your workout as you grow to be extra comfortable with the workout.

2. Schedule a ordinary time for exercise: Consistency is top to constructing a dependancy. Schedule a normal time every

day to your mindfulness exercising, and stick with it as a exceptional deal as feasible.

three. Make it a part of your daily normal: Incorporate mindfulness exercise into your each day ordinary, in conjunction with education inside the direction of your morning or night habitual, or at some stage in your journey.

4. Find an duty companion: Find someone who moreover cesires to boom a mindfulness exercising and decide to training collectively, or often take a look at in with each specific to live accountable.

5. Take a direction or workshop: Taking a mindfulness path or workshop can assist deepen your know-how of the workout and offer more help and steering.

6. Be affected individual and type to your self: Remember that mindfulness is a practice, and it's far natural to enjoy usaand downs alongside the manner. Don't be too difficult on yourself if you bypass over an afternoon or

have a hard practice. Simply famend it and recommit to your exercising.

By following the ones pointers, you may set up a regular mindfulness workout and maintain to gain the advantages of mindfulness over the years.

8. Cultivating a Mindful Attitude: Bringing Mindfulness into Daily Life

Cultivating a aware mind-set includes bringing the standards of mindfulness into every detail of every day lifestyles. This way being absolutely gift and engaged inside the gift moment, non-judgmentally and with an open mind. With a aware mindset, we will discover ways to approach our reviews with extra interest, openness, and reputation.

In this bankruptcy, we can discover techniques to cultivate a aware mind-set and bring mindfulness into everyday sports activities. We'll study a way to take a look at the ideas of mindfulness to each day lifestyles, and the way to apply mindfulness to beautify our relationships, paintings, and unique areas of our lives. We'll moreover discover how a aware mindset can help us navigate hard situations with more resilience and compassion.

By cultivating a aware thoughts-set, we can transform the way we revel in our lives, bringing more pleasure, due to this, and success to our each day testimonies. Whether we're washing the dishes, spending time with cherished ones, or navigating a difficult scenario, a conscious mindset can help us stay gift, engaged, and open to the opportunities of every second.

The importance of thoughts-set in mindfulness workout

The thoughts-set we supply to our mindfulness exercising is simply as critical as the strategies and physical games we use. Mindfulness isn't always pretty lots being present within the 2nd; it's also approximately drawing close to that second with a particular mindset of openness, interest, and non-judgment.

The mind-set we carry to our mindfulness exercising can substantially have an effect at the extremely good of our experience and our capability to domesticate mindfulness in our every day lives. Approaching our exercise with a curious and open thoughts can help us stay present, engaged, and receptive to some issue arises in the 2d.

Non-judgment allows us to test our reports without getting caught up in self-complaint or bad thinking, which could intrude with our capability to be gift.

A conscious mindset also can assist us expand extra self-interest and compassion.

By drawing near our research with interest and openness, we will discover ways to be aware patterns in our mind and behaviors, and discover them with more understanding and reputation. And with the resource of cultivating non-judgment and self-compassion, we can learn to be more type and mild with ourselves, even within the midst of difficult conditions.

In quick, the thoughts-set we deliver to our mindfulness exercising can significantly have an effect on our functionality to domesticate mindfulness in our every day lives.

By coming close to our reviews with hobby, openness, and non-judgment, we're able to growth a greater aware mindset that could help us navigate existence with greater ease and resilience.

Techniques for cultivating a aware attitude (e.G. Non-judgment, compassion)

There are severa strategies which could help us cultivate a more aware attitude in our every day lives.

Here are some examples:

1. Non-judgmental awareness: Practice watching your thoughts and evaluations with out judging them as properly or horrible.

Instead, try to undertake a impartial, non-judgmental stance and certainly look at your thoughts and feelings as they stand up.

2. Compassionate self-talk: When you be aware self-complaint or awful self-talk, strive converting it with compassionate and supportive self-speak. For instance, as opposed to questioning, "I can not try this," strive questioning, "I'm doing the first-rate I can proper now."

3. Gratitude workout: Take a couple of minutes each day to reflect at the property you're grateful for. This can help domesticate a more high-quality, appreciative attitude in the direction of existence.

four. Mindful listening: Practice in reality taking note of others with an open, non-judgmental thoughts-set. Try to avoid interrupting or considering what you are going to mention subsequent, and alternatively cognizance on in reality data the other man or woman's mind-set.

five. Loving-kindness meditation: This form of meditation consists of that specialize in sending love, compassion, and kindness to yourself and others. It can help domesticate a greater compassionate and empathetic attitude within the direction of yourself and those round you.

By training those strategies regularly, we will begin to domesticate a more conscious mindset in our every day lives. This can assist us approach our tales with extra openness, interest, and self-compassion, that can in flip assist us navigate life's traumatic conditions with greater ease and resilience.

How a aware mind-set can enhance common properly-being

A aware mindset will have a profound impact on our ordinary well-being.

Here are some strategies it could assist:

1. Reducing strain: A aware mind-set can help us manage pressure greater effectively via growing our attention of our thoughts and

feelings, and assisting us increase a extra non-judgmental, accepting thoughts-set within the path of them.

2. Improving relationships: By operating towards non-judgmental popularity and compassionate listening, we are able to decorate our relationships with others and growth a extra experience of empathy and expertise.

3. Enhancing self-recognition: A aware thoughts-set can assist us grow to be more attuned to our private mind, feelings, and bodily sensations. This extended self-focus can help us make greater intentional picks and take moves that align with our values and goals.

four. Boosting resilience: By drawing close to worrying conditions with an open, curious, and non-judgmental mind-set, we are able to cultivate more resilience and adaptableness inside the face of adversity.

five. Enhancing common well-being: A conscious thoughts-set can help us domesticate a more experience of not unusual nicely-being thru developing our feel of connection to the prevailing 2nd, promoting a extra tremendous and appreciative mindset closer to life, and fostering a extra experience of which means that and purpose.

Overall, a conscious thoughts-set can assist us increase a greater satisfactory and exciting relationship with ourselves and the area spherical us. By cultivating greater focus, compassion, and presence in our every day lives, we will revel in a deeper experience of peace, contentment, and motive.

nine. Mindfulness and the Brain: Understanding the Science Behind Mindfulness

As mindfulness has emerge as greater mainstream, scientists have turn out to be increasingly inquisitive about information the manner it influences the thoughts. Advances in thoughts imaging era have allowed researchers to gain new insights into the neurobiological mechanisms that underlie mindfulness, and to find out how regular mindfulness workout can trade the shape and function of the thoughts.

In this financial ruin, we are able to find out the fascinating area of neuroscience and mindfulness. We will delve into the fashionable research on the mind and mindfulness, and discover how mindfulness will have an impact on the mind in powerful strategies.

We may even communicate the neural pathways which are activated all through mindfulness exercising, and the way these changes in the mind can assist us to increase extra emotional law, resilience, and properly-being.

Finally, we are able to explore how mindfulness can be used as a tool for enhancing cognitive normal performance, creativity, and interest. By understanding the technological know-how in the back of mindfulness, we're able to deepen our exercising and gain a greater appreciation for the transformative electricity of mindfulness in our lives.

The neuroscience of mindfulness

In current years, there was an explosion of studies on the neuroscience of mindfulness. This studies has furnished new insights into the strategies that mindfulness can trade the form and feature of the thoughts, and how those changes can sell greater well-being and emotional law.

One of the important issue findings in this discipline is that mindfulness can growth hobby in the prefrontal cortex, a area of the thoughts this is related to hobby, selection-making, and emotional law. This elevated interest can bring about more authorities function, which refers to our capability to devise, prepare, and whole obligations.

Research has moreover tested that mindfulness can set off the insula, a location of the thoughts that is worried in self-recognition and empathy. This accelerated interest can reason extra emotional law and similarly empathy for others.

In addition, studies have demonstrated that mindfulness can change the structure of the brain. For instance, one have a look at decided that mindfulness meditation have come to be related to an growth in gray bear in mind inside the hippocampus, an area of the thoughts that is concerned in reading and memory.

Another examine observed that mindfulness meditation emerge as related to a lower in grey rely inside the amygdala, a vicinity of the brain this is concerned in worry and tension.

Overall, the neuroscience of mindfulness has proven that normal mindfulness exercise can cause adjustments within the mind that promote greater nicely-being and emotional law.

By data the methods that mindfulness influences the mind, we can deepen our exercise and benefit a more appreciation for the transformative energy of mindfulness in our lives.

How mindfulness changes the thoughts

Research has confirmed that everyday mindfulness workout can bring about structural and functional adjustments in the mind. One key region of the mind this is affected is the prefrontal cortex, that is liable for authorities functions which incorporates hobby, desire-making, and self-regulation.

Studies have discovered that regular mindfulness exercise can boom the thickness of the prefrontal cortex and beautify its connectivity with exclusive regions of the mind.

Mindfulness has furthermore been found to affect the amygdala, that is liable for the processing of emotions. Studies have proven that mindfulness exercise can cause reduced activation of the amygdala in reaction to strain and terrible feelings.

This can also offer an motive of why mindfulness has been determined to be effective in decreasing signs and symptoms of hysteria and melancholy.

Additionally, mindfulness has been observed to increase the activity and connectivity of the default mode community, it is associated with self-referential thinking and mind-wandering.

This may additionally moreover offer an explanation for why mindfulness has been decided to enhance interest and cognitive manage.

Overall, the studies indicates that mindfulness can also have a powerful impact at the structure and feature of the thoughts, principal to a big form of cognitive and emotional advantages.

How information the generation of mindfulness can beautify mindfulness exercising

Understanding the era in the back of mindfulness can enhance mindfulness exercise in numerous strategies.

Firstly, expertise how mindfulness modifications the mind can encourage people to exercising greater constantly. When people recognize that everyday practice can purpose structural and useful modifications inside the thoughts, they will be much more likely to stick with their mindfulness exercise and be patient with their progress.

Secondly, information the neuroscience of mindfulness can help humans apprehend how mindfulness works and the manner it may gain them. For instance, at the same time as people understand that mindfulness can lessen activation within the amygdala in response to pressure, they'll be more likely to use mindfulness to assist manage their strain.

Thirdly, records the technological information within the returned of mindfulness can assist people distinguish among effective and vain mindfulness practices. There are many unique strategies and tactics to mindfulness, and some may be more effective than others.

Understanding the neuroscience of mindfulness can assist people end up aware about which practices are much more likely to be powerful based mostly on the underlying mechanisms of mindfulness.

Finally, information the technological knowledge of mindfulness can assist human beings talk the benefits of mindfulness to others. When people can give an cause of how mindfulness works and the evidence inside the returned of it, they will be more likely to influence others to strive mindfulness practice themselves.

Overall, expertise the technological understanding of mindfulness can deepen human beings's statistics of the exercising and beautify their ability to use it successfully.

10. Bringing Mindfulness into Your Life: Creating a Personal Mindfulness Practice.

Mindfulness may be a effective device for lowering pressure, growing self-recognition, and enhancing famous nicely-being. However, incorporating mindfulness into each day life can be a assignment, specifically for novices.

In this monetary destroy, we will find out the way to create a personal mindfulness exercise that is tailored in your character dreams and manner of life.

We will cover topics which includes putting intentions, locating the proper time and place to exercising, and growing a routine that works for you.

By the surrender of this chapter, you can have the tools and expertise needed to create a sustainable mindfulness workout that allow you to cultivate more peace, joy, and presence in your lifestyles.

Creating a custom designed mindfulness exercise

Creating a custom designed mindfulness exercise can be a powerful way to deepen your information of mindfulness and integrate it into your each day existence.

Here are some steps to recall when developing a mindfulness exercising that works for you:

1. Set an cause: Start via the usage of clarifying why you need to workout mindfulness. Do you want to lessen stress, beautify awareness, or boom self-cognizance? Setting an motive will let you stay stimulated and focused as you develop your practice.

2. Choose a time and area: Find a time and place that works so that you can practice mindfulness. This is probably inside the morning in advance than you begin your day, in the path of a wreck at art work, or earlier than going to bed at night time time. The region have to be quiet, cushty, and unfastened from distractions.

three. Choose a way: There are many mindfulness strategies to select out from, together with conscious breathing, frame check, and loving-kindness meditation. Experiment with particular techniques to find out one which resonates with you.

4. Start small: Begin via practising for only a few minutes every day and regularly boom the amount of time you spend operating toward as you become greater cushty.

five. Find manual: Consider turning into a member of a mindfulness organisation or locating a meditation teacher who can assist manual you on your practice. Sharing your research with others also can help you stay recommended and engaged on your exercising.

6. Practice constantly: To revel in the entire benefits of mindfulness, it's miles important to exercising continuously. Even if you most effective have a couple of minutes each day, make the effort to exercising often.

Remember, mindfulness is a adventure, no longer a destination. Be affected person and compassionate with yourself as you growth your exercising, and recall that the advantages of mindfulness may be profound and lengthy-lasting.

Tips for staying recommended in mindfulness exercise

1. Set practical goals: It's critical to set ability dreams on your mindfulness exercise. This may additionally advise starting with only a few mins of exercising every day, and regularly developing your exercising time as you end up more cushty with the techniques.

2. Create a regular: Establishing a ordinary recurring for your mindfulness workout let you stay induced and dedicated. Try to workout on the identical time each day, and create a snug and inviting space for your exercise.

3. Find an duty partner: Having someone to proportion your mindfulness journey with let you live motivated and dedicated. Consider finding a friend or member of the family who is also interested by mindfulness, and take a

look at in with every distinctive frequently to offer beneficial resource and encouragement.

four. Experiment with particular techniques: If you locate yourself becoming bored or losing motivation collectively together with your present day mindfulness practice, try experimenting with specific techniques. There are many exceptional techniques to exercise mindfulness, such as frame test meditations, taking walks meditations, and aware eating practices.

5. Track your improvement: Keeping a magazine or a report of your mindfulness exercise will let you live stimulated and word your development through the years. Note any insights, disturbing situations, or changes you have a have a look at, and rejoice your successes along the manner.

6. Remember your why: Remind your self of the motives why you commenced practicing mindfulness inside the first region. Whether you are attempting to find more calm and rest, better sleep, or improved attention and

productiveness, preserving your goals in mind let you stay stimulated and committed for your exercise.

By incorporating the ones pointers into your mindfulness workout, you could stay inspired and dedicated, and revel in the numerous blessings that mindfulness can maintain to your life.

The blessings of a ordinary mindfulness workout and the way to stay dedicated to it.

A ordinary mindfulness exercise can motive numerous blessings for every highbrow and physical properly-being. Some of those benefits include reduced strain, expanded attention and productiveness, stepped forward sleep, and improved self-attention and emotional regulation.

However, no matter the first-class intentions, it is able to be tough to preserve a steady mindfulness workout.

Here are some pointers for staying inspired:

1. Start small: Begin with only some minutes of mindfulness workout every day and steadily increase the amount of time as your exercising becomes more mounted.

2. Be normal: Set apart a particular time every day in your practice and maintain on with it, even if it's only some mins. Consistency is critical to building a dependancy.

three. Mix it up: Try particular mindfulness practices, which encompass aware breathing, conscious movement, or conscious ingesting, to hold your exercise sparkling and interesting.

four. Find a network: Join a mindfulness business enterprise or find out a meditation companion to share your exercising with. This can offer guide, encouragement, and responsibility.

5. Be type to your self: Don't be too hard on yourself if you bypass over a day or your exercising isn't first-rate. Mindfulness is ready being gift and non-judgmental, so attempt to

follow that same attitude to your private workout.

6. Set desires: Establish precise goals on your mindfulness exercise, which includes meditating for a advantageous quantity of time each day or completing a positive variety of lessons in each week. Having a tangible aim to paintings closer to can assist keep you encouraged.

Remember, constructing a consistent mindfulness exercising takes time and effort, however the advantages may be transformative. Stay committed to your practice and be affected individual with your self as you still cultivate mindfulness in your every day life.

Mindfulness is a powerful device that permit you to reduce pressure, growth relaxation, and decorate normal nicely-being. By training mindfulness frequently, you may boom a greater enjoy of self-hobby, domesticate a more super mind-set, and enhance your relationships with others.

The strategies and bodily video games defined on this e-book will assist you to get started to your journey to extra mindfulness, and the technological knowledge within the returned of mindfulness can offer a deeper expertise of its blessings.

Remember that mindfulness is a exercise, and it takes time and effort to domesticate. However, the blessings of mindfulness are nicely genuinely clearly well worth the strive, and can truly effect each problem of your life.

By incorporating mindfulness into your each day recurring, you could create a extra feel of balance and concord on your life, and domesticate a deeper appreciation for the prevailing second.

Chapter 3: Mindfulness

What mindfulness is and what it isn't

Mindfulness is not a few elements you do and check off your list; it's far a manner of life. It's a preference to be aware, to be gift, and to show up as yourself without hiding or judging. It's moreover now not tied to any person faith or spirituality however accompanied through manner of way of humans of all faiths and beliefs to floor themselves, heal from trauma, and gather non-public increase.

Mindfulness is being conscious and present on purpose. Not to be harassed with meditation, that is a exercise that clears the mind. Mindfulness is first rate because of the truth you're aware of mind and present to them without clearing them and permitting them to cross clearly.

It can be a flowery intertwining of mind, however each mindfulness and meditation, at the same time as wonderful, are based totally definitely at the identical premise. They every sell self-recognition and help you connect with your inner most, innermost being.

Benefits of mindfulness

Anytime we take a second to sluggish the whole lot down, it will help drastically to lessen stress. It may even modify physiological abilties like coronary coronary heart charge and blood strain. Your interest, consciousness and mind feature can also furthermore growth as well.

Those who battle with tension and despair might also method mindfulness to adjust their feelings if you need to beautify their best of existence. Most those who be afflicted by highbrow ailments experience trapped and controlled. Learning to apply mindfulness as a tool can assist launch a number of that stress, allowing a person to experience extra emotionally sturdy.

We all have our coping mechanisms that we use to address the stressors of lifestyles. Some humans enjoy ingesting after which turn towards overeating, binging, or pressure consuming in times of trouble. Others dive into self-absorbed sports that push them faraway from their feelings and different human beings.

They are scared or ashamed in their feelings and consequently choose to dismiss their problems. Others select out negative behaviors till they in the long run hit rock bottom and realize they need help.

Mindfulness is a shape of wholesome coping mechanism. It is a tool in your toolkit to help control feelings instead of pushing them away. This way of lifestyles is a few aspect you could use everywhere and on every occasion. You aren't counting on an exercise fitness center or exercise mat.

The key gain is that it receives to the foundation of the problem. Mindfulness isn't a band-resource, however a scalpel. Though it sounds painful and might be every now and then, the blessings of digging deep a long way outweigh the harm we do to ourselves if we preserve to brush aside our ache elements and stressors.

Mindful 2d

Many advantages come from taking short conscious breaks at a few diploma within the day. Short conscious breaks will loosen you up bodily and emotionally, offering you with the electricity and courage to move on with anything you are handling that day.

Small, aware moments can be as clean as final your eyes for one minute and focusing for your breathing. Breathe in through your nostril and out via your mouth. You can depend your breaths, or actually pay attention and experience the air fill your lungs after which release.

Another easy mindfulness technique is to take a brisk stroll. This might also even be up and down a hard and fast of stairs in case you are going for walks and might't break out. Getting outside for 5 minutes to mention whats up to the solar and sense the easy air across your cheeks works wonders. It reminds you which you aren't by myself, and the area is huge and first-rate, masses large, and extra lovely than your issues.

I apprehend you can't manage the weather, but one aware second that everybody may also have is to have a have a look at and be aware of a smooth enjoy of rain. Rain is commonly a nuisance when you have made plans outside, have completed your hair a positive manner, or want to force somewhere. Rainstorms may be frightening or even volatile.

But what in case you stopped and skilled the rainfall for the primary time? Pay interest to the sounds, the smells, and the sight of it. Allow your self to be wrapped up inside the beauty of the phenomenon we take as a proper all of the time. Think approximately all the right the rain is doing for the earth, and for yourself. Pause what you are doing and get toward the rain to virtually experience it with out boundaries.

In this aware second, you're tuning in in your senses and letting yourself slow down to apprehend an act of nature. Rain has a tremendous smell because it drops into the floor in which the water mixes with the dust.

The sound of rain can tackle many workplace work relying on how speedy the wind is blowing or wherein the rain hits on the same time because it falls. Raindrops on the pavement sound brilliant from a tin roof or tree leaves.

Close your eyes and if you are brave, stroll round in it. Feel the drop in temperature around you or the take a seat once more of raindrops hitting your pores and skin. After you've got an immersive experience with a commonplace rainfall, you might be surprised about how grounded you experience in a while.

Human being vs human doing

Imagine a room full of children all carrying colorful garments. They are carrying headbands, hats, and socks with little bells that jingle when they stroll. Their satisfaction is plain on their faces.

On the opposite hand, they're additionally chewing gum loudly, speaking expressively with their pals and fidgeting their palms round continuously.

This is our life; Constant movement, and noises anywhere. Every time you switch spherical there are extra people who don't prevent doing or transferring and in no way appear to rest.

One of the exceptional subjects you could do for yourself is to surrender the perception that you could do all of it or have all of it. You are a character, and lifestyles is a gift. You are not what you do, and you aren't what you accomplish.

If we walk proper into a room and a person asks us to introduce ourselves, we can constantly speak about what we do. But what if we cited who we're? What we like? What our man or woman is like, and what makes us sense loved and at ease?

We are who we are on cause, and now not whatever we do or don't do will eliminate our intrinsic fee. It's important for us to speak reality and prefer to our minds and our our our our bodies. We accumulate this thru mindfulness.

Nothing is extra vital than loving your self and having the self perception to stand some thing comes your manner. Inner strength continues our heads held excessive whilst everything spherical us is falling apart. You owe it to your self to examine your great developments and apprehend who you are, not what you do.

Doing that comes out of being

But of path, we must "do." We want to paintings, deal with human beings, determine out what's for dinner and save you at the grocery to buy what we need to gain that. But in our doing, are we able to be non violent?

Can we live out each second with peace and contentment?

Being mindful at a few level inside the day is tough. Exactly one million matters distract us and staying focused is an Olympic feat. Mindful moments will help supply us lower once more to attention whilst we are losing it, and that's why it is vital to take short breaks.

Mindful moments are desired every on occasion, to reset and recharge. But for the duration of the day, we're capable of be aware of what's happening round us and in us.

When someone at paintings says a few factor, and we feel a ping in our hearts, we are capable of forestall and reflect onconsideration on that ping. What does it advocate? What emotion can I name it? Why does it damage, and what can I do approximately it? If not, then jot your self a phrase and don't forget it at the way home while you could leave the radio off, breathe deeply, and bear in mind of your emotions.

Mindfulness isn't commonly fixing topics inside the moment or understanding what they are. But it's far the act of paying interest, because of this that you don't have the luxurious of ignoring or stuffing emotions that upward thrust up.

Non-judging is an act of intelligence and kindness

If you are not in the dependancy of noticing how a bargain judgment comes into play as you have got mind and enjoy emotions, this facts can also come as a wonder. Every concept and emotion we've triggers a judgment.

We label matters as "accurate" or "terrible" pretty speedy. As quick as we label or pick out a few component, greater emotions and mind are added about primarily based mostly on that judgment. Things can get out of control if we don't stop and sit down with that first emotion in place of following the downward spiral.

As we study now not to select what consists of our mind as black or white, correct or terrible, up or down, and so forth; we're able to then use discernment to weigh the emotion or perception. This will bring about better picks and greater idea-out alternatives that have an effect on us and those spherical us.

Non-judging is an act of kindness because it allows for compassion and love. Non-judging gives us the gadget to mention the topics to ourselves that we might say to a loved friend.

When we make a mistake, non-judging permits us to evaluate the situation without throwing ourselves to this point below the bus in disgrace and remorse that it's difficult to tug ourselves again up. To have the courage to move beforehand and do higher subsequent time, we have to be moderate and type to ourselves.

Known mindfulness records

Fact #1: Mindfulness adjustments our brains for the better: Studies have tested that mindfulness can boom the gray consider utilized in our reminiscence, focus, interest span, or perhaps creativity.

Fact #2: Mindfulness can assist broaden empathy: Because mindfulness permits decrease the time in which we react to emotions, folks who practice mindfulness are better organized to deal with every different individual's emotions without judgment or harsh reactions.

Mindfulness moreover helps with choice-making and smooth questioning so we're capable of see a few different's factor of view and stories more genuinely.

Fact #3: Mindfulness can promote a top notch frame photograph: People who exercising mindfulness and splendid self-communicate revel in extra extraordinary frame attention and enjoy.

Because our society focuses intently on appearance and perfectionism, a few humans are tortured with the resource of manner of it. Mindfulness can help turn across the narrative and allow everyone to apprehend their our bodies in a modern-day way.

Myths of mindfulness

Myth #1: Mindfulness is a part of a religion: Most human beings suppose that high-quality folks that look at the religion of Buddhism exercise mindfulness. While many Buddhists use mindfulness as part of expressing their faith, every body with any faith can practice mindfulness.

Because it's far a manner of lifestyles, it does now not adhere to doctrine, theology, or pragmatic pointers. It is a manner of existence that every person who desires to attempt it can adopt.

Myth #2: Mindfulness is hard: While getting to know a few aspect new poses a assignment, developing a mindfulness exercising is possible. You can start with as low as one minute each day, absolutely focusing for your breath. This won't seem like a lot, however a hint goes an extended manner. If the "professionals" intimidate you, then take a minute to listing out all of the reasons you experience worried or inadequate.

Use this time to go into your self into the "amateur" category and permit your self off the hook. Even if it's miles difficult for you before the whole thing, with time, you may discover your rhythm.

Myth #3: You should recognize the entire day: While mindfulness is a few thing you could use throughout your day as a tool, it isn't always practical to apprehend each 2d of each day. Instead, bear in mind mindfulness as a checkpoint.

When you revel in careworn or need to check in together with your mind and frame, take a minute to reap this and workout mindfulness the usage of the ideas you may research under. Don't be too difficult on yourself and assume perfection however take advantage of the mind-set to help you be aware about what's taking location.

Myth #4: The cause of mindfulness is to be comfortable all of the time: While it is beneficial to exercise mindfulness and meditation to lighten up and be a remarkable deal a great deal much less confused, that isn't the most effective purpose. As you pursue mindfulness, you will be requested to be present together collectively together with your thoughts, emotions, and research. This might also furthermore enjoy uncomfortable and require you to cope with suppressed ache.

Attitudinal foundations of mindfulness exercise

Taking a step toward conscious dwelling is courageous and to be nicely-preferred. It is hard to choose out a way of life that opens you up greater genuinely to yourself and the arena. This may be terrifying in a manner. But as with each new adventure, we want to have our gear.

A hiker starting up to climb a mountain may want to have proper trekking boots, thick socks, a strolling pole, weather-appropriate garments, and a mild backpack. Just like a hiker, we can be prepared too.

Here are seven attitudinal foundations to help you set up a mindfulness exercising. Keep in thoughts that you'll be studying approximately some of those for the number one time, so have grace and staying energy with yourself as you navigate this ordinary territory.

Non-judging

We are so connected to judging that we don't even comprehend that we're doing it. Our minds categorize every revel in as each exquisite, poor, or indifferent. This is an automatic reaction that we need to find out. Sometimes those judgments assist us, however now not each time. The everyday judging can emerge as overwhelming and vain.

Going into mindfulness with an focus of the way an entire lot we decide our thoughts, feelings, and moves will help us understand and undergo in mind the effort and time we positioned forth into judging. It can be surprising. The concept isn't always to stop judging all of the time but to hold our judgments cautiously in our arms like a porcelain doll and take a look at them. Consider. Question. Be curious. And then slowly release if want to be.

Our behaviors are related to our thoughts, emotions, and values. In adolescents, behaviors are praised or criticized, so something conditioned us to react to the manner we had been dealt with over the years, and as our brains boom, we are able to assume and act for ourselves. Many adults spend hours in treatment untangling the strings of messages they've heard their whole existence and are data virtually now.

Non-judging is essential due to the fact a few belongings you revel in or be given as genuine with approximately your self can also without a doubt be someone else's projection on you. It's vital to maintain in thoughts what rises in us and in which the supply is. When you are working towards mindfulness, and also you sense a strong emotion upward push, prevent the response. Consider, question, and be curious approximately that emotion and your herbal subsequent response. Be quiet to your innermost self and apprehend the judgment that you vicinity at the emotion, the reaction, and your self.

With time, you may are seeking out out possibility strategies to manner through and address your emotions, mind, and judgments. It is important to exercising non-judging for your mindfulness practices, as it will free up deeper truths for your self.

Patience

It's no thriller that humans have extra problem with patience on this speedy-paced worldwide. We nurse our ego loads that watching for nearly something feels unjust. We don't like to confess how impatient we are, but it is the fact.

We just like the concept of endurance, and we all need extra. But we battle via the vital steps to become a more affected person individual. Mindfulness is an excruciatingly affected person manner of existence. Your egocentric inclinations will yell at the top in their lungs at the way to circulate on, however conscious workout will educate you to stay in it and preserve breathing.

Patience isn't honestly anticipating something; it's retraining your frame and thoughts not to be right away glad. Progress does now not are available in a pill. In order to be a more affected person, kind, slight, and easy-going character, the artwork is each day and might sense daunting.

The first-rate manner to exercise endurance is to sluggish down. Think approximately taking location a stroll with a small child. They are interested by the maximum minute info, and you may roll your eyes while they invent you but some extraordinary rock however aren't they the happiest?

Doesn't that fifth rock thrill them to no forestall? We don't ought to be satisfied with rocks, however we're capable of practice noticing the little subjects. A small toddler has no cares inside the international, no bills to pay, or automobiles to pressure to appointments.

Children use their tiny arms to find out and stay curious. Walking along them at their tempo will do wonders for our personal boom. How are you able to slowdown on your life proper now? How are you capable of "forestall and heady scent the roses?"

Beginner's mind

When you begin your mindfulness journey, having a beginner's thoughts is important. You have to clean your head of preconceptions and mind. You can be considering every exclusive character's adventure and the way they method their conscious way of existence.

While it's beneficial to recognize how others embody mindfulness, you'll method it for your manner. Everyone has a unique fashion and character that brings mindfulness to lifestyles in a beautiful manner.

Let's take the stress off. Having a newbie's thoughts method you're open to what mindfulness will recommend to you. You are willing to try new topics with out worry. Although you'll be concerned about selecting what works for you and what doesn't, it's critical to accept as right with that you will get there in time. Trial and errors are the name of the sport, and that's not anything to be ashamed about.

Beginners are excited and feature plenty to check. But they may be additionally brilliant listeners who are not jaded with the aid of enjoy. As you walk into this journey, hold an open mind, and take note of what mindfulness is putting in up for you. What gets you excited? What new matters do you need to strive?

When someone mentions "aware riding" or "aware consuming," and you don't understand exactly what which means, experience the jolt of interest and satisfaction that flows thru you.

Pick up books and magazines and test on-line articles to help you acquire greater statistics. You have already made a high-quality preference in reading this e-book to assist open your worldwide to all of the possibilities. If you experience overwhelmed via all of the alternatives, then sit down down and make a listing of wherein you experience maximum lively to start. Start there, and with time, you will be helping others along in their mindfulness journey.

Gratitude is a superb region to begin at the same time as starting the adventure. You won't enjoy capable of even explaining what mindfulness way to you even as you are really in the beginning degrees. But try to be thrilled about the little tidbits which you are getting to know.

The greater you look at, the clearer matters will be to you. You will pick out and choose out out your favorite strategies and first-rate practices as a manner to benefit you in your cutting-edge-day season of life. Have religion, everyone starts offevolved as a newbie first.

Trust

An entrepreneur CEO of a enterprise will constantly be extra invested within the enterprise than the employees. Self-hired commercial enterprise organisation owners who began with not anything and constructed an empire will inform you how loads blood, sweat, and endless tears had been worried. No one is aware about the company and commercial organisation like the person who created it.

No one cares about it as plenty both. Only the proprietor who has been there considering that the begin is as invested emotionally, financially, and mentally.

It is the same with you. You are the simplest you inside the worldwide. There is not any awesome you. No one is aware about your thoughts, coronary heart, soul, and frame higher than you. Every strain detail, each reminiscence and painful photograph from your past sparks something in you that others can't feel.

It might also revel in which include you dont aggregate in with the area, or don't have some thing to provide. You are wrong; the area dreams you to expose up as your proper self because of the fact no person else can take your vicinity.

Now think about this; do you take delivery of as actual with yourself? Do you agree with your intestine instincts and feelings as they wash over you? Or do you 2nd guess the entirety, wondering that in all likelihood you're wrong and there's no need that lets in you to figure subjects out in your own?

Mindfulness calls in case you want to open up and take delivery of as true with yourself in a deeper manner than you have got before. Your frame is making an attempt to tell you subjects, and it desires you to pay interest. It needs you to realise that there are more profound topics occurring than you will in all likelihood comprehend at face fee. With time, you can determine and tackle one difficulty at a time as you agree with yourself through the approach.

As you take a seat with your self and move about your day, be aware of how often you throw your self under the bus or question your very personal options. Think approximately the idea of those accusations. Are you having second mind because a person else does things otherwise? Or you might be ashamed of who you're? If appropriate, go with what you feel strongly about, and don't appearance once more.

Non-striving

We have dreams and measures of success that we're continuously checking in with at some point of our lives. It's smooth to try to push for that subsequent level, the exquisite advertising and advertising, the proper frame, or maybe a more peaceful mind-set. We need to change matters, development, glide in advance and located the past within the lower back of us.

That type of rushed living is not healthful. It goes another time to the fact which you are a character, not a human doing. It's important to set apart your striving if you need to make real progress. Don't be fooled via way of a to-do list with boxes checked off.

Think approximately what striving has finished to you. Reflect for your years and recollect how striving in your personal or expert lifestyles might in all likelihood have damaged you. Maybe your physical health has been affected. Or, perhaps your emotional fitness has taken a success.

Without judging yourself or your past options, have a observe the motives behind your striving. Are you in search of to prove some aspect? What are you attempting to show, and to whom? Others? Yourself? Letting pass of striving isn't always giving up for your dreams.

It's clearly moving your desires to consist of your fitness; bodily, intellectual, and emotional. If striving has now not served you inside the beyond, recall how you could stay mindfully in a way that permits you to reap your desires without sacrificing some component valuable.

Imagine yourself at artwork or at a place in which you have always driven yourself to the boundaries. Maybe it's the fitness center wherein your self-hatred comes up and talks to you negatively, beating you up as you strive to finish a exercise. You surrender the exercise feeling extra defeated than energized due to the voices to your head.

Let's approach the fitness center with a non-striving attitude. Think about your dreams as you stroll into the gym, via the doors, and to your preferred nook. You set your topics down and take one last sip of water. You breathe and think about what you need to carry out this time. How is it terrific from last time? Your literal goal can also moreover but be the equal: walk or run at the treadmill for half of-hour.

But what if in preference to beating your self up for buying worn-out speedy, you installation ordinary intervals to walk? And on the same time as you're taking walks, you repeat mantras and inspire yourself. You thank your body for its difficult paintings and the present it's miles to you. If you've got got were given terrible mind, you renowned them with out judging and rewrite the narrative in a type and mild manner.

Acceptance

Acceptance may be pressured with approval, and therefore this idea can be tough to understand on the start. We need subjects to decorate and be better, so why ought to we "take shipping of" the way we're? Wouldn't that surrender?

You can though have desires and thoughts of the manner to broaden in my view, but mindfulness calls you to humble your self, and get maintain of in which you are right now. When you are listening to your thoughts and frame, subjects might also moreover arise which you warfare to include as actual. You might also furthermore speak it away, want it away, or blame someone or some factor else. However, the wholesome step is to appearance yourself for who you're in the meanwhile and be kind except.

Acceptance allows you're making authentic trade. It's now not healthy to brush aside a coronary coronary heart hassle. Your first step is to get scientific assist and make a plan to move ahead. It's the same aspect with our emotional and intellectual fitness. When our our our our bodies supply information, we need to pay interest and receive what our bodies are telling us. It's the primary course of motion.

It's difficult to invite for help, and it's difficult to admit while we are wrong. Acceptance is like raising your hand in a study room whilst the teacher asks who desires after-university tutoring. It might humiliate you to confess which you need to stay after university and redo the problems on the worksheet that the entire elegance have already got end up in. But to get an tremendous grade, you have to be sincere with your self. If you try too difficult to preserve up appearances, you will probably end up cheating or lying to your parents.

When you admit and take transport of that you need assist, you recollect the remarkable about your self. Because you comprehend that with difficult paintings, attempt, and braveness, you can do higher.

Letting bypass

We have come to the give up of the seven attitudinal foundations of mindfulness, and that is the very last one. Non-judging permits you practice letting pass of judgments for every single idea and feeling. It permits you to launch the stress to location subjects into instructions.

Patience is needed to allow go of the rush momentum we revel in in a quick-paced global. As we approach matters with the eyes of a toddler who is curious and now not in a hurry to get someplace, we allow bypass of desires and goals that don't imply a top notch deal to us.

Having a newbie's mind is a first-rate way of letting circulate of the heightened choice to be an expert. We can be loose to strive new things at the same time as now not having to be on the pinnacle of the beauty.

Establishing a healthful receive as real with with ourselves encourages us to permit glide of the concern and lies that say we aren't appropriate enough. We shed what has dragged us down for see you later and as an opportunity maintain to the intestine instincts and splendor we can discover in ourselves. As we undertake a mind-set of non-striving, we permit pass of our location within the rat race of lifestyles. Non-striving is a gift to us that we're capable of't have except we allow circulate of to-do lists that aren't getting us anywhere.

Chapter 4: Beginner's Thoughts

Who am I? Questioning our personal narrative

It sounds crazy to talk about the voices on your head, but every person have them. We can hint phrases again to our childhood or even as in recent times due to the fact the previous couple of years. There are positive things that we inform ourselves time and again, and that will become our internal narrative or our "story."

Brené Brown tells us to observe the recollections we're telling ourselves in her e-book, Rising Strong. She encourages us to speak the reality approximately the story we agree with and to share that reality with the ones we love.

"The story I am telling myself" opens us up to admit what we don't forget inside the 2d, and it normally is the worst-case scenario. The tale isn't normally constructing us up but tearing us down. The story can be appearing out of disgrace and guilt or believing a person else is wondering the worst human beings.

So, ask yourself, who am I? What are the recollections I am telling myself and believing? When you enjoy maximum willing, what mind are digging deep tracks for your mind? What track is on repeat?

Pay interest to those. We will dig into what we're able to do with them. It's adequate or even endorsed to impeach the narrative that defines our life. When you have got were given been in university, perhaps you were the quite one, or the smart one or the smooth-going one.

Maybe people depended on you, and also you felt you could in no way allow them to down, so that you just went with the waft in preference to putting forward your self. Narratives can exchange with time, and perhaps you have decided your self in a modern-day-day story after years of being a person else.

A new method or relationship or segment of lifestyles need to ship you spiraling into possibility reminiscences which may be in addition harmful.

It's essential to be aware of the subjects which can be on repeat. Our brains get stuck in cycles, and it's tough to break out of them. Your internal narrative will provide an reason behind subjects the manner it has normally interpreted them, in step with your story.

For instance, allow's say you have end up ready for artwork, and you could't discover the proper outfit to place on to your large presentation. You choose one outfit, however the colours seem too bold, and you consider the way you used to get made amusing of at university for wearing brightly coloured and slightly obnoxious garments.

Every outfit you select out up makes you revel in insecure because it looks as if "an excessive amount of," and then you definately surely pay attention your self repeating frantically on your mind, "You are definitely too much."

It's difficult to regain self perception and pick the right outfit even as wheels out of your past are spinning so tough you could't pay attention whatever else.

You are more than any narrative

So, what will we do?

First, we calculate the accuracy of the internal narrator, the tale, and the tracks laid. Is it actual? Where did it come from? Does it assist me in any respect? Most of the time, the internal narrator isn't always beneficial. You can upward push above beyond activities, past wounds, and past lies which you have believed for way too lengthy.

You are more than any narrative. You are a totally particular and delightful person who has extra to provide this global than what you're giving your self credit score score score for. Mindfulness calls for you to do a little paintings, however. You need to reset the tracks.

Celebrate the coolest and exquisite subjects approximately the struggles you're presently having. Referring again to the closet state of affairs as you put together for artwork, consider how we can rewrite that narrative. Instead of thinking of yourself as "an excessive amount of," how are we able to reframe that?

We can famend that growing up; our style choices were loud, modern, and colorful. Others did now not commonly understand it, but you've got been attempting your superb and having fun.

So, allow's take that fun into your closet and rejoice your creativity with an outfit that has a pop of coloration but tasteful quantities to maintain a expert photo. Let's say you select out black pants, a impartial top, however a headband with smooth tones of springtime shade to suit your vibrant character.

As you step out to art work, you're refusing to accept as authentic with the lie that you are "too much." You are believing the high-quality about your self and rising above the narrative. It's vital to your pleasant outlook to embody your creativity and show it in doses that deliver you delight and make you experience most like yourself.

With time, you can alternate your narrative as well. If you become stylish and perhaps a touch over the top, perhaps you can discover that during distinct regions of your existence. Try a interest that allows you to faucet into that wild, colourful issue. Art, song, pastimes, and literature can intensify who you are and assist you to not get embarrassed about it however encompass it!

You are complete

One of the lovely subjects about mindfulness is that it brings you to a focus which you are a whole person with price and countless well without a doubt well worth. The narratives we tell ourselves beat us down.

They convey out the horrific whilst what we want is a whole photograph of our correct, lousy, and unpleasant. Mindfulness does not beat back our missteps or troubles. It certainly teaches us that we're whole, critical, and particular beings simply as we are.

Mindfulness permits us to get in touch with a entire sort of feelings. Think of your capability for emotions, mind, feelings, and sensitivities. It's huge. We can revel in the bottom of lows and the very wonderful of highs in a count of mins, even seconds. Your complete and complete being consists of complexities that experts have been reading and will continue to check all of the time.

Understanding and believing your complexity will assist liberate the guarantee that nothing is a mistake. You are entire even at the same time as you enjoy you are lacking some issue. Everything you need is at your fingertips. What's unexpected, and what many human beings take years to decide out, is that the greater you pour out for others, the extra whole you revel in.

What you provide is what you get. Mindful days hold our cognizance on our intrinsic properly truely worth and charge in all its complexity, and this is some thing as a manner to allow the negativity to fall away like fats off the bone.

Beginner's mind

One way to domesticate a beginner's mind and increase more healthful wondering styles is to live curious. Instead of immediately beating ourselves up for terrible thoughts and behaviors, we also can need to ask questions instead.

Let's say you visit attend a meeting at paintings or at your infant's college. Someone in price says some thing that makes you irritated. The nice technique may be to dig into that feeling. You can ask your self, "Why am I feeling this way?"

Explore with interest rather than focused and excessive negativity. Think about the scenario from a newbie's attitude. What if this grow to be my first assembly, and I knew little approximately the most important or the govt.? How may additionally want to I way the revel in then?

This may moreover appear overwhelming, however the goal is to disarm yourself. Take away the weapons which might be hurting you. If you have lots taking location on your thoughts that you could't separate matters from every different, it is able to be time to step over again and placed on a sparkling pair of glasses.

Liz Forkin Bohannon talks about hobby in her ebook, Beginner's Pluck. She says that hobby will much more likely make you greater a success as you ask yourself questions in area of creating declarative statements.

With questions, we're in an open posture and organized to research and exchange. Having a novice's thoughts is ready being open and willing to alternate, so hobby enables us with this.

She additionally says that asking questions will dig deep into why you're doing what you are doing and will also assist you have a look at your ardour in the first place. It motivates you to make a alternate. You want topics to show out higher, so you ought to tweak how you have were given have been given accomplished subjects in the past to trade the very last outcomes.

As we ask ourselves questions and live curious, we're capable of remedy our very very own issues in a miles extra immoderate extremely good way. The subsequent time you face a brick wall (in advance than you get too discouraged), click on on on on the lightbulb of hobby.

Brainstorm the techniques you've got were given treated this earlier than and think about what you can do in a one of a kind way. Make a small adjustment and strive again. Don't beat yourself up about the beyond. Simply switch something up to look if it makes a difference.

Nothing incorrect with thinking

One assumption about mindfulness is that to do it proper, you need to flip off your thoughts sincerely. Many humans find that exceptionally difficult, simply so they sense like failures proper off the bat. It's tough to take a seat although, pay attention, and installation our mind.

But it is a fantasy that we have to turn our brains definitely off at the equal time as we exercise mindfulness. Our mind isn't evil. We don't want to run away from it. The goal is honestly to pay attention to our thoughts.

It's crucial to circle back to the attitudinal foundation of non-judging. These mind that come into our minds need to be taken into consideration but no longer judged. We don't want to criticize ourselves for having those mind. It's like we're tasting a ultra-present day fruit for the number one time, and lots of mind soar up as the feeling of the fruit slides round in our mouths.

The flavor buds are telling us a few issue. We can embody interest and discover this new enjoy without judging our mind. If we don't locate it impossible to resist, ask why. Is it bitter? Too tough or too clean? Is it much like a few element else we devour? Is the feel or fragrance throwing us off? Why?

We can educate our minds, much like we teach a brand new domestic dog. It takes exercise, strength of will, and cognizance. There are undesirable thoughts that allows you to are available, and we have to lead and gently guide them a ways from us and replace them with new mind which can be right and useful. In order to head inside the direction, we need, we want to sit down with our mind first. We can't overlook approximately them or address them harshly in advance than we even have a danger to determine out what they recommend.

It can be an awful lot less tough in mindfulness to have a look at the encircling subjects externally. The breeze outside, the sound of a own family chatting as they walk past you, or birds flitting round on a spring day.

You can focus for your breath and definitely take in your surroundings. It is greater of a assignment to have in mind internally. Thoughts enjoy so invasive, so abrupt, that it is able to be a warfare to weigh them.

Begin with the idea that your thoughts are not right right here to damage you, however they're right right right here to teach you some component, and this is why we need to pay interest.

Befriending our questioning

If we do now not establish our mind because of the truth the enemy, it's a natural next step to befriend our thinking as we exercise mindfulness. These mind are, no matter the entirety, part of who you're.

They can also moreover moreover want modifications, however we're capable of technique them with gentleness and kindness to allow down our guard a bit bit. Defensiveness will no longer assist us bypass ahead with our dreams and dreams.

Draw near your thoughts and approach them like an antique pal. Using interest, ask the questions softly as we're reading to treat our mind kindly and with sensitivity. Mindfulness is prepared watching and non-judging, so we need to deal with our thoughts with a beneficiant mind-set.

If you're within the center of a mindfulness workout whilst your thoughts wanders, attempt no longer to have a bad reaction for your mind as although it has completed a few thing wrong. Figure out why your mind wandered. Get to the muse of the problem.

Work on coordinating additives of your mind; like your thoughts, emotions, and then moves. Find out how they're related and why your mind works the way it does. It sounds complex, however the artwork is definitely really worth it.

Focus at the prevailing 2nd

As we approach our thoughts with kindness, we are capable of permit bypass of the beyond and the future. The amazing part of mindfulness is that it specializes in the present. What a lovable way to live this life, 2nd through the usage of using moment.

As we take note of the thoughts and feelings we've got have been given, it's clean to leap to conclusions or need to trade things right away. But persistence is essential to staying within the moment. What are we able to look at proper now thru paying attention to what's proper in the front of our faces? Friends, the opportunities are endless.

We spend a awesome deal of our existence planning for day after today. We have retirement plans, artwork dreams, circle of relatives tour thoughts, and bodily health aspirations. Most people are, unfortunately, not satisfied with their current us of a of existence. Society is continuously pushing us into the next day in advance than we've got juiced these days for all its well well worth.

Gratitude can assist us live within the gift and convey our mind-set lower back to what we had been given rather than what we want to show up in the destiny or what we need to change approximately our lives. A gratitude mag is a wonderful mindfulness workout as it continues your eyes at the now.

Your gratitude magazine may be a thick notebook with gold-lined paper, or the again of the grocery list from this morning's errands. Sit down with a pen and as you are taking deep breaths, listing a few matters from the very last 24 hours that you are thankful for. I need to keep a short time body because it allows to keep us in the 2nd.

We can search around and see the topics that make us happy. It may be a small aspect, much like the easy breakfast you cherished, your preferred house plant, or the way the moderate falls into your living room at sundown.

Or it can be people that deliver you exceptional pleasure. Think about some key moments within the very last day that filled your coronary coronary heart with peace. Embrace the tiny bits of affection that fill you up and offer you with the power to keep going.

The present is a present. It sounds cliche, however it is foundational to mindfulness. When we rush through this existence, the people round us reach out to touch us, but we're already long beyond. How critical it is to be gift to ourselves, those we like, and the adorable global we stay in.

Now is usually the right time

As we live in the present 2d, the reasons to live up for exchange begin mounting up. There are continuously such a lot of things to exchange that it is simple to get frozen and have "evaluation paralysis." When this takes area, we push off taking movement thru reading all the reasons it's truly now not the ideal time.

It will in no way be the appropriate time, just so makes it the proper time!

If you wait too extended to make a change for what you experience passionate about, the passion will placed on off, and it will be hard to gain momertum. Start with being conscious of your goals and recall the subsequent logical next step.

Go for a stroll outdoor and, as you breathe and recognize your surroundings, recognition on one intention you keep in mind you studied you may tackle. Clear away any judgment or awful self-speak and decide on one or movement steps you could take right away: like in recent times. Don't wait.

We can get in our very personal way of fulfillment and development via convincing ourselves that topics will really get better. Or our problems will go away on their personal. It may be tempting to take the easy way out and do not whatever.

But being aware desires honesty, and being sincere with ourselves will lead us to the ones next steps. We have to have the self notion and braveness to take those next steps with the useful resource of the use of the attitudinal foundations said proper right here.

"The gift 2nd is the excellent time over which we have dominion."

Thích Nhất Hạnh

What a beautiful manner to view our lifestyles, particularly those who are recuperating manage freaks. We have the prevailing 2nd, however we can't control the future. There are, in reality, many stuff which may be past our control.

Mindfulness is not approximately control. It's approximately liberating and letting bypass of manage. But that doesn't recommend we want to overlook about the stewardship placed in advance than us. The time we were given is supposed for use.

Trapped within the past or living in the present

One Harvard have a look at observed that we spend almost half of our wide awake time with a wandering thoughts, dwelling on both the beyond or the future.

Wow. Half of our extensive unsleeping time. That sounds approximately right. We bear in mind our past frequently, trying to avoid pitfalls or heal from reports. And some of us will be predisposed to stay within the future, planning and scheming and hoping and having a pipe dream approximately what's coming.

So how are we able to pass on from the past? How can we get "unstuck" from what has been dragging us down?

The beyond is drastically powerful, as we can view things in hindsight. Events and events are over, for efficaciously or horrific, and we're capable of test them with easy eyes. The trouble is our emotions are typically involved at this kind of deep degree that we revisit the beyond time and again like a torture chamber. Parts oldsters understand how essential it's far to be loose from our beyond, but it's addicting to transport over scenes and feelings over and over.

If you have got suffered trauma for your beyond, counseling and treatment may be a outstanding assist. Licensed therapists are prepared with gadget and strategies to guide you to a higher region mentally, emotionally, and physical. There is surely no disgrace in getting help in case you are locating yourself deeply rooted in beyond events which may be crippling your gift lifestyles.

Therapy may be significantly painful. It can also sense every so often like your coronary coronary coronary heart is being ripped out of your body. It's furthermore a huge dedication and might occasionally take years to artwork thru all of the troubles. Many could attest that it is beyond nicely well worth it. Opening your self to real healing can set you on a trajectory in the course of a whole lifestyles.

We have skilled haunting matters in our past that we need to conquer to live within the gift. Many people warfare to move on and embody their modern-day lifestyles once they have heavy and traumatizing pics from their past on repeat in their minds.

After you get help to heal out of your past, you may use the mindfulness exercise of reputation to encompass who you're, which encompass your past. Whether it is painful recollections because of your picks or others' alternatives compelled upon you, accepting your reality is top to a whole and healthful lifestyles.

How To Stay In The Present Moment

Living in the present has emerge as a need on this busy worldwide, and most oldsters do now not understand a manner to stay in the present; Here, we've got listed some strategies to help you start the system.

Focus On Your Body

The first manner to be in the 2d is to focus in your frame. Be greater in tune with all the bodily sensations you sense thru your body inside the present second. Also, try to pay attention to and contend with your body's desires. Try to pay attention from head to toe and silently be privy to your body.

Start your day right!

We are all continuously in a rush at times in existence; Instead of waking up in a horrible united states and leaping some distance from mattress, why not make an effort for yourself at the same time as you wake up? Take a deep breath and try to recognition on your self and your surroundings.

Don't forget about to take a couple of minutes out of your time table and exercise mindfulness. It will allow you to live in the 2d.

Conduct a aware body scan.

One of the most useful mindfulness sports activities you may do is frame scanning, which assist you to to live in the present 2d.

The gadget:

Lie nevertheless to your returned.

Try a few deep respiration sports activities sports to come to be aware about your frame.

Be privy to your body; Try to popularity on how your garments revel in on your body and the manner small subjects feel in contact with you.

Try to focus at the factors of your frame that damage you.

Focus on every a part of your frame, from your ft in your head.

Write a journal

Journaling is an excellent method for studying to stay in the 2nd and is also one of the most famous intellectual health sports sports.American creator Julia Cameron uses one of the journaling techniques called "morning pages."

Before heading on your workspace, take a couple of minutes to open your mag and begin writing. There's no incorrect way to put in writing down the morning pages. All you have to do is write three magazine pages; with out overthinking, write down the whole thing that comes for your mind.This is truely one way to maintain a mag; You can choose diverse distinct strategies, including log turns on and others.

Start unmarried-tasking

It's clean to burn out while you multitask, which influences your conventional regular overall performance and the wonderful of your art work.

A single venture lets you work greater efficiently. It can help you recognition on your self and be greater gift. Try to set up a single venture on your life, no longer satisfactory at the same time as you paintings but moreover while you do small things like looking TV, reputation at the TV in place of the usage of your cellular phone simultaneously.

Concentrate in your respiratory.

Staying focused and controlling your respiratory is one of the most critical additives of meditation, which helps you to live in the gift 2nd.

Focus truly to your respiration and do that whilst final your eyes and sitting within the lotus role for better concentration. Feel the air flowing into your frame and the air flowing out with every breath. Better recognition and attention also can help quiet your thoughts and provide you with peace.

Focus on what is in the front of you.

Most people get lost on the same time as speakme to a person or maybe analyzing or searching a few element. Focus on what is going on inside the the front of you in choice to drifting off into an imaginary international.

Practice conscious meditation

Mindful meditation is one of the maximum well-known strategies to discover ways to stay inside the gift second and turn out to be more grateful, preserve peace of thoughts, and manipulate anger.

In intellectual health improvement sports, meditation performs a considerable function. It lets in increase mindfulness via manner of manner of developing interest and calm inner us. Consider taking day trip of your busy time desk to try to meditate; You can try and recognition on the phrase "now" throughout meditation.

Spend time in nature

Spending time in the presence of the splendor of nature is one manner to learn how to be within the gift 2nd effectively. Walking outside permits you interest higher to your existence, and strolling additionally permits lessen your strain and anxiety via releasing endorphins.

Reduce your enter

Sometimes we overload ourselves with a number of work and recognition on 1,000,000 matters. In such times, it could make sense to shorten your contribution.

Instead of checking your e-mail or social media as soon as you wake up, lessen your input, and focus on what is happening round you. Also, do now not overexert your self at paintings; maintain your mind freed from litter. This dependancy can help you grow to be conscious on your every day lifestyles.

Try chanting mantras

Singing mantras are generally applied in meditation to boom interest and discover ways to stay within the gift second. You can chant multiple mantras, as every life-style and area has mantras in its language.

Try sitting within the lotus posture and chant your mantra. This smooth system will help quiet your thoughts, reduce stress and anxiety, and popularity on the existing 2nd.

Try doing yoga

One of the numerous tremendous equipment to floor yourself is yoga! Yoga includes the maximum flexible sports activities with masses of blessings. It lets in people suffering from depression and unique highbrow ailments. Yoga moreover permits you to enjoy yourself and your body and to attach them to the prevailing 2d. Yoga additionally allows you learn how to be in the gift second by way of manner of focusing on your breath and thoughts.

There are many yoga poses that you could do; Even in case you are new to yoga, there are smooth yoga poses like Sukhasana, Vajrasana, and others so that it will can help you get commenced out.

Enjoy in which you're

Each parents wants to construct a higher destiny, and there can be not some thing wrong with that, however in constructing your destiny, do now not break down your present. According to Eckhart Tolle, "Expectation is extra of a country of thoughts than a state of affairs we discover ourselves in," which means that if we need to accumulate a few thing in life, we have to appearance ahead to it. Still, on the alternative, it is based upon totally on what we want to understand.

For instance, ask someone sitting at the bus save you what they are doing. Most of the time, they will reply that they'll be looking forward to the bus, but what if, as an alternative, they reply that they will be sitting and respiratory the fresh air and looking what is going on round them? Here you may apprehend the difference among perceptions and the way it influences our lives.

By in reality changing your mind, you may begin appreciating the prevailing greater. To understand how to be in the present 2d, we need to first fee and revel in the present for what it's miles.

As Buddha stated, "Don't live at the past, do not dream of the future, recognition your thoughts on the prevailing moment." What subjects maximum is whether or not you live your existence or are in reality passing with the aid of the usage of.

Set Intentions

Mindfulness requires a chunk of planning. Like some problem, you will now not have fulfillment or improvement in a single day with simplest a snap of your fingers. If you are a habitual individual, placing an intentional time of the day to practice mindfulness will assist you build up the modern addiction.

You need to take a walk after artwork every day, through your self or with pets or family contributors. Pay interest to what's occurring round you.

Grab the gratitude magazine we cited in advance and jot down a few subjects in the morning or at night time time time. Keep it with the aid of the usage of your bed so that you can begin your morning and cease your day on a immoderate high-quality note.

Use your planner to set goals. Each week, don't forget one manner you'll be more conscious. Maybe that's setting apart electronics in the direction of lunch or dinner and deciding on to recognition for your meal. Or no longer taking note of music or a few issue on your pass back and forth. Set an alarm to your cellular telephone for as soon as an afternoon or perhaps as speedy as an hour to take quick breaks to simply breathe and recenter yourself.

Schedule a larger, longer set of time every now and then for a mindfulness retreat, undertaking, or event. This can be a time of painting or paintings challenge, even if you aren't an artist. Or a morning to live in bed journaling, studying, and resting. Everyone dreams a highbrow health damage each every now and then!

Using the muse of non-judging, set less expensive intentions, and don't be afraid whilst you don't pretty get it right. Mindfulness is education a manner of existence, and there may be so much room to enlarge. You can take baby steps now, and with time you can see that you have made widespread development.

Kendra Adachi writes in "The Lazy Genius Way" that she set a cause of doing yoga every day to decorate her mindfulness and flexibility. But at the same time as the purpose modified into too large, she failed. So as a substitute, she took the quite courageous approach of placing the vicinity's tiniest intention.

Starting on January 1st, she decided to do one yoga characteristic every day. It turned into the downward canine pose. It took her seconds, but a few days she even managed to do it two times! Because her purpose modified into too small to cease, she spent the 365 days and past doing yoga each day and has positioned the small alternate really advanced her properly-being.

Your intentions do now not need to be large. In fact, it's probable better if they aren't. You understand yourself, so choose a few factor manageable for you at this diploma of your lifestyles.

Spend time with thoughts and emotions

Everyone is aware about relationships expand while you spend extraordinary time collectively. You can't get to understand someone except you are speakme and sharing, starting off in vulnerability, and being honest with each other.

It's the equal manner with ourselves. We need to spend time with our mind and emotions to get to recognize them, and via that, we will live in touch with ourselves. Just like a relationship, we cannot forget approximately ourselves and expect to broaden.

As we live a aware existence, we are going to stumble upon thoughts and feelings which may be uncomfortable, specially with our beyond and the way we experience approximately activities that came about years ago.

It's vital in those moments to lean into the difficult. Good matters will come from a little little little bit of digging. It will take time and braveness, however the greater time you commit to this essential work, the greater it'll assist you ultimately.

Don't be afraid to take your self out for espresso and dive into what makes you tick, what ticks you off, what you need out of lifestyles, and the way you can make it seem. Ask yourself the difficult questions and use the device we have cited to gain a better attitude and make an movement plan.

Therapy also can assist immensely with the complicated mind and feelings that upward push up. Sometimes it's crucial to get an impartial 1/3 party to weigh in on our maximum difficult conditions.

There are conclusions that we may not have get right of entry to to besides, with vulnerability, we invite a person else to look into our lifestyles occasions and recommend with love. It doesn't even have to be formal remedy. A appropriate buddy who is aware about us properly could probable assist us see from a one-of-a-type perspective.

After you communicate with a person, ensure to come back lower back lower back decrease again to your self and type out your mind and emotions again. Journal or do a on foot meditation to open your self up. Breathe deeply physical, however also deliver your frame vicinity to respire metaphorically too. If you keep speeding through lifestyles, your mind and emotions won't get the space they want. And you don't want to lose contact and float too speedy to the following factor with out addressing what's taking place deep in your coronary coronary coronary heart.

What does liberation from suffering suggest?

Humanity is whole of suffering. To be human is to go through in a unmarried manner or every other. Some humans have endured extra suffering than any human must ever be subjected to. It will wreck your coronary coronary coronary heart.

Accepting pain and suffering is to end up liberated from its outcomes. Yes, we're able to suffer and war all through this existence. Pushing ache and suffering away and ignoring or stifling it will not help us cope with it.

Part of the freedom that incorporates mindfulness is permitting your self to encompass your struggles. You don't must need them or maybe like them however try now not to show your head away.

Self-compassion is a beautiful manner to deal with the ache and struggling that has encounter in your lifestyles. Not handiest are you acknowledging the hard area that you discover yourself in, however you're respiratory life and wish into the state of affairs in desire to negativity. Have grace with your self. Have patience with yourself. Talk for your personal coronary coronary coronary heart as if you had been comforting a toddler.

Liberation from struggling does no longer advise that the ache and struggling will go away all of the time. It just method that you don't need to stay inside the prison of it. By accepting it, you are being real to your self, and that gives you freedom.

Liberation is inside the workout itself

Imagine being on pinnacle of a cliff and looking for on the land below. The sky feels the most essential you've got had been given ever felt on your existence, and beauty surrounds you. The bushes and their leaves, the wispy clouds within the sky, and the kiss of the wind to your face captures your hobby.

You are there with all that makes you, you. Inside your body might be bodily ache, or inner your coronary heart is probably brokenness that you aren't positive will ever heal. You are wearing weights, and you need to be free.

Chapter 5: Awareness

Do you positioned that a few factor as clean as focus can unencumber mindfulness for you? As you're reading approximately mindfulness, you would possibly pay interest lots about being aware.

Imagine you are experiencing a loss of a relationship. It can be a breakup, a friend that moved away, or a loss of life. In your moments of surprise and grief and passing via specific degrees, how conscious are you of what's taking place?

Are you in touch with how your body feels and how every emotion feels as they flood you at a few degree within the day and night time time?

Awareness lets in you, within the midst of ache, to revel in ache otherwise. Freedom comes with popularity because you're mastering about your self and spotting what your heart, body and soul may be going via.

We are so used to flying past our emotions, explaining them away, or doing our incredible to healing them right away. However, if we are alert to ache as it comes up, we are able to peer with expertise into our gift times.

Awareness will not do away with our pain. If you've got suffered a lack of a courting; your feelings are deep and layered. You aren't proof against ache actually due to the reality you are extensively self-aware.

You can pick out small strategies to carry reputation into your life as you're studying what it's miles. Living existence on this manner lets in us to stay with extra openness.

We stay maximum of our lives on autopilot, doing the same matters time and again with out actually thinking about it. We without difficulty jump out of the triumphing moment, and this breeds dissatisfaction. As you workout focusing on one difficulty at a time, you'll increase your mindfulness and recognition.

It may be anxious to remind yourself when you enjoy the familiar slide to pop decrease back into cognizance. Be slight and sort, slowly transferring your mind lower back to the prevailing. Look. Feel. Be. Check in with your self, and with time, your capability to stretch out your conscious moments will expand more potent.

Think of cognizance as an out of doors stress. It's not similar to questioning and feeling. It lies beyond that border. Awareness holds and consists of your thoughts and emotions, but it does no longer control them.

Don't try to trade the entirety that recognition is defensive. You can watch your thoughts and feelings without being sucked into the swirl of them much like the violent storm they are able to sometimes be. Create separation.

A Place to Sit by means of Kabir

Don't skip outside your private home to appearance vegetation. My friend, don't problem with that excursion.

Inside your frame there are flowers. One flower has a thousand petals.

That will do for a place to sit down. Sitting there you may have a glimpse of splendor inside the body and out of it, in advance than gardens and after gardens.

This poem with the resource of Kabir is a adorable instance of the way a good deal capability we've indoors of us ready to be unearthed. Think approximately the flowers and petals which you preserve interior you, along all of the complicated mind and emotions. Awareness holds onto the whole lot so that you can usually generally tend to your self like a garden.

Inhabiting focus

We all recognize that demanding does not trade our instances. So why are we able to do it? Why can we so desperately need manage that we've convinced ourselves that demanding approximately a few factor is truly worth our time?

It's clean to say that we shouldn't fear or maybe tell others no longer to worry, but however the mins and hours we spend on topics we will't manage is baffling.

If we ought to inhabit hobby, making it part of our every day lifestyles, then we leave no room for fear. If hobby is a field that holds our thoughts and emotions, then we will lightly nudge worry out of the way so that it doesn't input the box.

All we've got were given is the instant we're in. No one is assured even their next breath. So, each breath then can be considered a miracle, a blessing, a risk to be thankful. We are so frequently taking even our very breath without any consideration.

So how do you inhabit hobby for your life? How can you are making it a exercise and addiction that works together along side your life-style?

The first goal is to be aware. That sounds stupid; of route, you are huge conscious. But many zombies thru lifestyles as despite the fact that they're napping, and a good way to now not bring about a fulfilling existence. Awake yourself to what's happening in and round you. With careful mindfulness, hold in thoughts the mind and feelings you keep to your attention box.

Some thoughts or emotions can be very painful to you. Other mind are matters you have got been pushing away. Being conscious is residing with eyes massive open to what your lifestyles approach. It manner carefully considering what has occurred inside the beyond without judgment.

If a few thing is genuinely too painful, widely recognized that and circle lower again to it later. But don't nod off to it, therefore ignoring the trouble. With time, you may summon the braveness to confront the scariest components of your self or your past.

The second motive is to inhabit your body. Allow attention to circle via your bodily body and be aware about what rises to the ground. Tensions can lie in the shoulders, stomach, returned, or head. Focus and hold right away to what your body is making an attempt to tell you.

Too frequently, we forget about what our body is trying to inform us due to the fact we have turn out to be so used to the vessels, we have lived in for such pretty a few years. Sometimes our bodies are shouting at us, and it's important to pay hobby. You can't inhabit consciousness in your intellectual lifestyles if you aren't aware of the crucial symptoms your physical frame is giving.

The 1/three goal is to cast off distractions. Many matters want our hobby, but we want to be aware and on pinnacle of things. How would you sense if a few element terrible took place because of the fact you weren't paying hobby? It may moreover plague you with guilt as you recognize you may have prevented it.

Think about how commonly every day you're distracted, multi-tasking, and centered on multiple factor. At art work or at home, it may be poor, and our common performance will lower if we are able to't stay targeted.

Relationships also want first-class time, and even as we're pulled in too many commands, it is able to reason tension and frustration. With exercising, we will live aware and aware in every state of affairs, each dating, and every situation of the day.

Taking care of this moment

This second is a present, and you ought to in no manner neglect approximately it. As you look returned in your existence, reflect onconsideration on moments or relationships you took without any consideration on the same time as you have got been in them. Have you out of place a person that intended a few thing to you? Do you remorse the time spent with them, no matter the truth that it turned into difficult? Of path not. A life whole of relationships is complicated, and it will be higher to cope with each moment like a valuable present to be cherished in choice to like a disposable item for use, thrown away, and proper away forgotten.

Inner frame attention

What is the inner body?

The time period "internal frame" describes a go along with the drift of existence that nourishes your bodily being. As you benefit notion into its space, you connect to the supply of advent. In brief, inhabiting your inner body slows the tempo of your thoughts and brings mental and emotional stability.

Your internal body is the formless, non-physical part of you. It has no boundary and is positioned under the outer regions of your frame. This strength brings your physical self to existence. Here you can revel in the power flowing inside the confines of your pores and pores and skin.

Tune into this feeling and align together together with your inner body. To illustrate, keep in mind charging a cellphone. Watch because it involves existence and completes its obligations. Life strength works in the same manner for your body. In this analogy, the cell telephone is your body, and the electric present day-day is its strength. Once you may experience this subtle strength, your focus will boom, this cause is the end result of connecting together with your internal body.

Your physical frame is an organic gadget containing many structures and ranges. Each of these takes vicinity in splendid layers. Their floor consists of pores and pores and skin, muscle mass, and bones. There are cells, fluids, tissues, and organs at a deeper stage. Thought and emotion provide an explanation for the subtler degrees of form. Each of these layers paperwork the general profile of your body.

Explore their nature and experience how they revel in. This shape of examination puts you extra in touch with the internal frame. As a quit end result, your thoughts will become a smart and beneficial tool, and its movement can not weigh down you.

In truth, conscious area creates and holds every item within the cosmos. To accomplish this reason, it works via all of your cells. This mind is the internal body that works on your human stage. When you song into this, your thoughts and emotions come into balance.

What occurs even as you experience the internal frame?

When you enjoy your inner body, its power is activated. This movement strengthens your frame's life pressure, which nourishes everything at the mobile stage. That's because of the truth you get higher quicker, don't age as brief, and function fewer diseases.

Your frame is an clever tool that has the electricity to regenerate and heal itself. It takes region through the cooperation of many tissues, fluids, and cells. Each of those entities in your body is a aware and realistic being.

They use their minds to connect and paintings with many one of a kind systems. This act desires both interest and nutrients to live on and thrive. Without such popularity, your physical skills visit pot. It is then tough for them to heal.

When you grow to be aware about your inner frame, you deliver interest into your cells. It prevents undesirable thoughts and illnesses from accumulating to your location. Let's take the case of an owner who leaves his house to show how this works. What takes place to their residence within the occasion that they don't flow lower back after some years?

Dirt and particles are in all likelihood to build up in its partitions. The constructing rapid falls into disrepair, and uninvited visitors invade.

Otherwise, intruders and debris are lots a good deal much less probable to enter even as someone is home. It keeps the residence strong and intact. Likewise, as you connect to the inner frame, your degree of popularity increases.

A higher degree of popularity creates region for the healing of the mind and frame. In fact, your cells have become extra spacious and in a rustic of equilibrium.

This movement prevents extra intellectual power and pollutants from constructing up to your frame. You will quick discover ways to decorate your existence and fitness. The give up end result is a lot much less sickness in the thoughts, body, and spirit.

How does the connection with the internal frame have an impact on your thoughts?

Connecting with the inner body strengthens, expands, and opens your mind. This hobby permits you to talk with the space and know-how of lifestyles. You gain internal energy, nicely-being, thoughts, and answers.

The size of space and statistics is found in you. These allow your complete being to live effortlessly and balance. Believing which you are your mind blocks get entry to to that intelligence. By merging with the internal body, you learn now to see past the outer crust of your thoughts. This imaginative and prescient gets rid of all intellectual blocks blocking off area and statistics inside you.

A strong foundation of cognizance ensures that your mind and moves are not unstable for your properly-being. Imagine building a tower on a flat base of unfastened sand. The tower might not live there for prolonged. Now trust the identical shape constructed on a solid, deep concrete base. The building remains strong — regardless of ground adjustments or weather conditions.

In this situation, the tower indicates your mind; its base is your internal frame. A strong grounding in this base permits for a robust inner electricity, well-being, and a more focus of existence.

An alert and regular mind boom as you end up more privy to your inner frame. From that 2d on, not anything receives past you, no matter what takes vicinity. When you live on this stillness, perception and idea get up. You then connect to the source of advent and recognise that existence is one. This insight comes on the identical time as you connect with your internal frame.

How do you exercise inner body reputation?

You train to be privy to your internal frame by using manner of way of being but first. It is then smooth to revel in your emotions and feelings. See if you can experience existence under your pores and pores and skin. As you spend 3-four weeks in this workout, thoughts need to have less strength over you as your focus will boom.

The following steps will help you switch out to be more aware about your inner strength subject. It is critical to understand that they may be clues and act as courses. With this goal, there are not any suggestions even as running in the direction of. It permits to try each trick and locate the only that works nice.

Sit snug.

Sit and make yourself comfortable on the floor or in a chair you're resting on. When you are prepared, near your eyes. There isn't any need to maintain yourself in a rigid posture. The maximum critical detail is which you use the least amount of attempt to assist your posture.

Remain as calm as possible.

A harassed frame shows a hectic thoughts. When you preserve your frame nevertheless, the thoughts turns into a whole lot less noisy. It becomes more privy to this exercise. In addition, a strong frame requires the mind to gradual down the rate of its mind.

Watch your respiratory.

If you find out it smooth, convey your interest to the movement of the breath. Start with the aid of taking a deep breath in and softening your cognizance as you exhale. When it's miles tough to attention, don't forget a brilliant recuperation moderate surrounding you. With each breath, visualize the breath in this slight. Allow this slight to fill all of your region.

Take care of your chest hollow vicinity as it fills with air and the lungs empty. As you exhale, relax your efforts to manipulate your respiratory.

Become aware about the sensations for your body.

You will feel moderate and subtle sensations as soon because of the truth the body relaxes. These encompass moderate tingling, tension, pain, and heat in one-of-a-kind locations. Observe a mild electric powered sensation on your limbs and thoughts.

Here is a moderate and nourishing strength that beats your coronary coronary heart at the same time. Notice how the blood moves and flows from the middle of your coronary coronary heart thru your torso. This act of announcement lets in your body to loosen up.

Draw attention in your frame, neck, and head.

Now that you are in track with the frame, discover each issue. Start collectively in conjunction with your toes. Spend ten seconds on every and be aware how you feel. Feel your ft, legs, torso, neck, palms, and fingers. Then direct your interest on your entire being. Appreciate all reactions transferring thru your area. Recognize the electricity and presence that deliver your form to existence.

The mind will try and distract you with this workout. As this takes location, word all of the mind and questions that come to the floor. Keep returning for your popularity point each time you word this happening. Don't fear if you locate it difficult to pay attention during this exercising. Understand that that is a quick-time period workout to increase your cognizance. Because of this, you do now not must stress your self to be perfect.

Notice the power your frame is keeping.

Imagine your body is a hole vessel. Is it clean or hard? Stay with that recognition and discover it together with your senses. You will fast revel in the subtle power in and around your pores and skin. Continue with this experience so long as you enjoy cushty.

How can the technique of internal frame reputation be summarized?

To summarize, the technique of noticing your inner frame: be nonetheless, loosen up, after which check your sensations and senses. When your mind wanders, please deliver it decrease lower back for your interest element. This exercising will assist you increase a extra clever mind and a healthful body. With this foundation, you could results allow cross of undesirable thoughts.

Do records and interest exist within the body?

Every cellular, tissue, and fluid to your frame has knowledge and attention. These capabilities thrive beyond the confines of your pores and skin. The practice of being together along with your frame opens the door to this idea. Such quiet focus sustains and animates all that exists. See its impact in nature, in which the scope of lifestyles is countless. As quickly as you revel in this motion, your entire lifestyles adjustments.

Every mobile for your body is connected to all existence energy. Within you, this imaginative and prescient is prepared to amplify and blossom. To recognize this, spend numerous minutes a day noting this power. Understand how it brings your body to existence. By doing so, you awaken inner records and expand as a person.

This motion modifications your mind, your health, and your lifestyles. Soon you may have an extended-lasting reference to the mind of existence. You will gain this aim after a few weeks of practice. From there, you may stop the attention bodily video games and start to launch your mind. In short, this model changes your complete life.

Chapter 6: Anchoring

Mindfulness anchoring techniques; Anchoring frame to stay present all of the time

Mindfulness uses many strategies, and taken into attention actually one among them is known as anchoring. Anchoring lets in us to test in on ourselves and stabilize. Anchoring encourages you to stay gift constantly.

Anchoring is about focusing your interest on simply one element. If you grow to be distracted, you may redirect your mind again to that one aspect. Often our mind wanders because its project is to hearth thoughts at this type of rapid speed that we will't ever preserve up.

So much like dog strolling footwear use regular strategies to train the animals to pay interest and obey, we are able to commonly and kindly anchor ourselves to construct that muscle reminiscence.

Why is it vital to live gift? Regret comes from not residing our existence to the fullest, and lots of be troubled via regret. The splendid gift we are able to supply to ourselves is to be privy to the winning 2nd and now not run a ways from it.

All of nature lives inside the second. The wood, the ocean, the animals. We can studies lots from them, as we ought to. Children clearly have a way of now not disturbing about the future but residing greater carefree lives. What if we without a doubt embraced the winning for what it's far without wishing it away?

There are many strategies to anchor your self with a purpose to live present. Breath is the most not unusual manner to anchor oneself. It is with you all the time, it is natural, and includes motion. What's moreover excellent about breathwork is that it is something tangible to which you may keep on.

You can place your fingers by way of your factor, in your chest, or belly. Our breath can frequently emerge as shallow and too much inside the top chest. The cause is to train ourselves to respire with our belly. Deep respiration also combats the combat-or-flight response that surges even as we experience threatened. It moreover fills the body with oxygen which we need to stay.

When you prevent what you are doing and consciousness or your breath, it will ground you. Involve all your senses; feeling, being attentive to, connecting to the relaxation of your body. Notice how your chest moves and your stomach fils up as you breathe in and deflates as you breathe out.

Breathing offers you another threat each few seconds while your thoughts wanders. It's a reminder that it's a workout, and also you get to strive once more, and once more, and yet again. Breathing deeply and that specialize in that single act will help to calm you, regulate your emotions, and clean your thoughts of all the clutter.

If you need a specific method at the same time as respiratory, right here are some.

1. Box respiration is even as you breathe in thru your nostril for 4 seconds, keep the breath for 4 seconds, breathe out via your mouth for 4 seconds.

2. Alternate nostril breathing: The first way you can do that is thru using keeping your dominant hand like a fist under your nose. Use your thumb to close your right nostril and inhale. On the exhale, launch your thumb and use the knuckle of your index finger to shut your left nose.

The second manner can be to relaxation your index and middle finger on your brow between your eyebrows. Alternate your thumb and knuckle of your ring finger to close each nose at a time on the identical time as respiratory deeply and exhaling.

3. Long exhale: Some may be aware that it is easier to inhale longer than to exhale. Spend a couple of minutes focusing on the exhale, respiratory out longer than you probably did earlier than, and seeking to empty each

ultimate breath earlier than inhaling over again.

Be cautious no longer to push yourself. It's now not healthful to try to accumulate everything. This isn't about proving yourself or pushing the bounds however focusing on your breath or an object to move in the direction of mindfulness.

If you want to study some thing, focus your eyes on one component while doing a respiratory exercising or near your eyes if you are feeling overstimulated. You may even combine respiratory with mantras.

Anchoring with mantras empowers you with super mind and grounds you to the truth. This is a fluid opportunity you can use at the go to recenter your self mentally.

Here are a few mantras that you could test out to locate what works for you. "I am" statements give you manage, but a mantra can be created with a few element you need to verify to yourself.

You can begin them with: I can, I want, I will, I certainly have, and so on.

1. I am cherished.

2. I don't need to chase a few element.

3. I accept as true with the device.

4. I am affected person and kind.

5. I am wherein I want to be.

6. I am grateful.

7. I am unfastened.

eight. I am lovely.

nine. I am well worth it.

10. I can growth and studies.

Sometimes one word can cause you to loosen up and enjoy associated with your self. Love. Hope. Peace. Truth. Grateful. Heart. Family. Beauty. Safety. Patience. Now.

You can use the chant to circle lower lower back to at least one notion as you practice mindfulness. Say it aloud or to your head. Combine this with respiratory and connecting to your self.

Connecting the thoughts and frame is fairly vital in mindfulness, so a frame test is one manner to paintings through every element of what makes you, you.

When acting a frame experiment, you need an open thoughts and coronary coronary heart, just like some thing else on your mindfulness journey. You are virtually watching and bringing attention on your physical body without judgment.

Emotions and mind will really come and can be overwhelming but use your body as an anchor and recognition on the subsequent a part of the check.

Either mendacity down or sitting, begin at the bottom of your frame. This exercise is utilized in Jon Kabat-Zinn's education software for mindfulness-based-strain-cut rate which treats illnesses and continual ache.

Start at the side of your feet and foot on one thing, and waft up in your leg. The motive is to hobby your mind on each part of your body, listening to what it might inform you. Focus for a few seconds, then flow into on through your mid-phase, torso, and palms, and cease with the face and head.

Allow reminiscences to flood you as your mind discovers and explores every a part of your body. Give appreciation wherein it's miles due, word pain that cries out softly or loudly, and think about not absolutely your bodily coronary coronary coronary heart however the studies and feelings you frequently feel deeply in your coronary heart.

It is beneficial to ground ourselves to the our bodies we use every day for masses capabilities. A frame test can cast off darkness from regions to which we've have been given given little attention and understand problem spots. A shorter body test, every mendacity down or sitting, is also beneficial.

If you don't want to commit to an entire-body check, mendacity down and paying attention to your body for a couple of minutes also can help you relax. If you do that mindfulness exercise in advance than or at bedtime, you could fall into a more comfortable sleep.

Target precise areas of your body which you need to hobby on. If you be bothered with the resource of complications, neck pain, or again ache; attempt to loosen up the ones muscle businesses thru breathing in and out slowly and bringing deep peace to the ones areas.

Jon Kabat-Zinn says on net page 153 of his e-book, Wherever you bypass there you're,

"We talk of damaged hearts, of being hard-hearted or heavy-hearted, because of the reality the coronary coronary heart is understood in our culture due to the fact the seat of our emotional life. The coronary coronary coronary heart is also the seat of love, satisfaction, and compassion, and such feelings are in addition deserving of hobby and of honoring as you discover them."

He encourages at a few stage in the body test and mendacity down mindfulness moments to understand the body additives as physical however moreover metaphorical. What does the coronary coronary coronary heart constitute? Your throat and voice? Your intestine? Not handiest do our our our bodies carry out great, great obligations every day, but a few elements constitute a few factor deeper as well.

Morning time is a tremendous manner to anchor yourself and begin your day ride right. Though we are connected to sleep and require an terrific night time's relaxation, even getting up a couple of minutes in advance inside the morning can enhance our mindfulness.

Greet the day with out your cellular telephone, pc, TV, or maybe the newspaper. Greet the DAY. The sun (if it's far up but), the despite the reality that air, the quiet residence, your quiet soul. Breathe deeply the usage of one in every of your chosen strategies and wake your mind, body, and heart as much as all of the possibilities to come back again to you that day.

It's been proven again and again that gratitude and the appreciation of existence itself does wonders for our highbrow fitness. There can be masses to fear about due to the fact the day progresses, but inside the morning, in advance than the push begins offevolved, take advantage of the time to anchor yourself.

"Morning is once I am awake and there can be a sunrise in me…" Henry David Thoreau, Walden

If you're a glass-half-complete form of person, you may already enjoy constructive approximately what anchoring, and mindfulness can do for you. You may additionally get excited about the excellent benefits, but you would in all likelihood simply have a tough time coaching your self to lighten up.

With time, the ones bodily sports will growth on you, and you'll pick out your favorites. If you are a glass-half of-empty shape of character, it might take greater time to get used to living in the gift and paying attention to what's taking region on your body and thoughts. Stick with it. Don't give up.

Mindfulness delivered to all of the senses

Our five senses are an truely terrific manner to participate in being human in this earth. Touch, scent, flavor, sight, and being attentive to are stunning gadgets that permit us to hook up with ourselves, with every other, and the sector spherical us. Mindfulness takes benefit of the sensory opinions and offers us some element to latch onto as we stay big wakeful and alert.

www.ingramcontent.com/pod-product-compliance
Lightning Source LLC
Chambersburg PA
CBHW071444080526
44587CB00014B/1982